Presented
to

_____

on

_____

The Baker
Book of
Bible
People
For Kids

The Baker

Book of
Bible
People
For # Kids

Terry Jean Day

Contributing Editor
Daryl J. Lucas

A DIVISION OF
Baker Book House Co

How to Use
the Baker Book of Bible People for Kids

You know baseball cards, right? This is a book of baseball cards, except it tells about Bible people, and nothing but Bible people, instead of baseball players. It gives the important stats and details on each of the "players." It gives the highlights. It tells who these folks are and what they did.

Most adults might call these biographies. That'll do too.

In other words, if you want to know about the most valuable people in the Bible, read this book. It gives the inside track on just about every Bible person who ever did anything.

Two Kinds of People

You'll find two kinds of biographies in this book: long ones and short ones. The long ones tell about the people who did many or important deeds. Moses, David, Mary, and Paul shine in this spotlight, along with 46 others. Each of these men and women either lived a long time doing what God wanted, or did it very well, or both. Some of the Bible's biggest villains also get this kind of top billing.

The short biographies tell about the people you might call minor characters. They don't show up in most lists of "great Bible people," but they show up in the Bible. And they get more attention from the Bible writers than just a name in a list. They did something important once, or they saw something important happen, or they helped a major character. Recognize any of these: Miriam, Abigail, Joseph, Onesimus? If not, you should. These folks played key roles in the lives of Moses, David, Mary, and Paul.

95109

The Details

The short biographies have four parts. Here's an example:

1. Name
> Zacchaeus (zuh-kee-uhss)

2. Biography
> Zacchaeus was a chief tax collector for the Romans who became a follower of Jesus. He was a Jew and very rich. Among the Jews, tax collectors were seen as traitors because they worked for the Roman government. Not only did they take money for taxes, but they took extra for themselves. Jesus went to Jericho where Zacchaeus lived. Zacchaeus was a short man so he climbed up a sycamore tree to see Jesus as he passed by. Jesus went home with Zacchaeus. Jesus' love for Zacchaeus turned Zacchaeus' heart to God. Zacchaeus gave half of his riches to the poor. He also paid back four times the amount he had cheated from others.

3. Bible References
> See the story of Zacchaeus in Luke 19:1-10.

4. Key event
> Jesus' ministry

The long biographies have six parts—the same four parts as the short biographies, plus two more. Here's an example from Aaron:

5. Relatives
> Brother: Moses
> Sister: Miriam
> Sons: Nadab, Abihu, Eleazar, Ithamar

6. Study Questions
- What message from God did Aaron and Moses give to Pharaoh? (Exodus 5:1-4)
- How did Aaron and Miriam criticize Moses, and what happened to them? (Numbers 12:1-16)

Pronouncing the Names

Don't feel bad if you don't know how to pronounce a person's name. Just look at the part in parentheses. Here's an example from Zacchaeus:

Zacchaeus (zuh-**kee**-uhss)

The part in parentheses tells you how it sounds. Say the bold part loudest.

That's it! The Baker Book of Bible People for Kids isn't hard to use, just fun and packed with information. It's here for you any time you need to learn about a Bible hero or villain. We hope you like it.

May God bless you as you study his Word.

Terry Jean Day and Daryl J. Lucas

Aaron (air-uhn)

Aaron was the brother of Moses. God used Aaron and Moses to speak to the people of Israel. The two brothers also spoke to Pharaoh (king of Egypt) and showed him signs of God's power. Aaron then helped Moses lead the Israelites out of Egypt. Aaron also became the first high priest of God. But while Moses was on Mount Sinai talking with God, Aaron listened to the people instead of obeying God. They were impatient because Moses was gone so long. They wanted a god they could see. Aaron melted their jewelry and made a golden calf as an idol. God punished the people for worshiping an idol.

See Exodus, Leviticus, and Deuteronomy 1–10 for all of Aaron's story. See Hebrews 7:11 about the priesthood.

Key event
The Exodus

Relatives
Brother: Moses
Sister: Miriam
Sons: Nadab, Abihu, Eleazar, Ithamar

Study Questions
• What message from God did Aaron and Moses give to Pharaoh? (Exodus 5:1-4)
• How did Aaron and Miriam criticize Moses, and what happened to them? (Numbers 12:1-16)

Abel (ay-bul)

Abel is the second son of Adam and Eve mentioned in the Bible. Abel was a shepherd. When he brought an offering from his flock to the Lord, God accepted it. His brother Cain was angry because God did not accept his offering of farm crops. In jealousy and anger, Cain killed Abel. He was the first human being to die and the first person ever to be murdered. In the New

Testament, Abel is called "a righteous man" (Hebrews 11:4). Jesus warned the Jewish leaders that they would be responsible for the blood of all the righteous people from Abel to Zechariah.
See Abel's story in Genesis 4:1-8. See Jesus' warnings in Matthew 23:35 and Luke 11:51.

Key event
Creation; Garden of Eden

Abiathar (uh-**bye**-uh-thar)

Abiathar was a priest during King Saul's reign. He served with his father, Ahimelech. Saul had all the priests killed for helping David. Only Abiathar escaped. He fled to David and told him everything King Saul had done. Abiathar became the spiritual leader to David. Later Abiathar helped David take the Ark of the Covenant to

Jerusalem. While David was king, Abiathar supported him. But later, when Solomon became king, Abiathar supported Adonijah (another of David's sons). Solomon made Abiathar leave the priesthood and return to his fields.
See Abiathar's story in 1 Samuel 22:6–23:13 and 1 Kings 1:1–2:27.

Key event
Reign of Saul and David

Abigail (ab-i-gale)

Abigail was the wife of Nabal, a wealthy but foolish man. David and his men had protected Nabal's workers from bandits. At sheep shearing time the workers were celebrating. David sent his men to ask for a gift of food. Nabal was rude to David's men and sent them away emptyhanded. In revenge, David planned to kill Nabal and his whole household. Abigail sent a large gift of food to David. Then she went and apologized. She wisely asked David not to do something wicked for which he would be sorry. David thanked Abigail for her good advice. Later, Nabal died and David married Abigail.

See Abigail's life in 1 Samuel 25–31; 2 Samuel 1–2; and 1 Chronicles 3:1.

Key event

Saul's reign; David fleeing Saul

Abijah (uh-bye-juh)

Abijah, also called Abijam, was the son of King Rehoboam and Maacah. His father appointed him to be the chief prince among all the king's sons. When King Rehoboam died, Abijah became king. Abijah ruled for three years. He followed his father's poor example and sinned against the Lord. But once in a battle against the king of the Northern Kingdom, Abijah turned to God for help. He taunted his enemies and encouraged his own troops. He and his men called out to the Lord. God gave Abijah the victory.

See Abijah's life in 1 Kings 14:31–15:1–8 and 2 Chronicles 11:20; 13:1-22.

Key event

Abijah's reign

Abimelech (uh-**bim**-uh-lek)

Abimelech was a son of Gideon and of Gideon's slave girl. Abimelech decided to make himself king. He went to his mother's brothers and asked them for help. So the men of Shechem gathered around Abimelech. They helped him kill Gideon's 70 other sons. Abimelech killed all his half-brothers, except for Jotham, who escaped. Jotham told a parable to the people. He said that Abimelech and the people of Shechem would destroy each other. Three years later, God punished Abimelech for murdering his brothers. Abimelech was killed by a woman in Shechem who dropped a millstone on his head from atop the city wall.

See Abimelech's story in Judges 8:30, 31; 9:1-57.

Key event

Time of the Judges

Abishai (ab-i-shye)

Abishai was one of David's nephews. His mother was David's sister Zeruiah. His brothers were Joab and Asahel. He was also an officer in David's army. Abishai was known as the chief of the Thirty and a hero. He was a bold fighter who killed many of David's enemies. He was fiercely loyal to David and once saved his life. He even would have killed King Saul for David, except that David stopped him. David did not want to be responsible for Saul's death. He waited for God to judge Saul.

See the story of Abishai in 1 Samuel 26:1-13; 2 Samuel 2:18– 23:19.

See other mentions of his family and his bravery in 1 Chronicles 2:16; 11:20; 18:12; 19:11, 15.

Key event
Reigns of Saul and David

Abner (ab-nur)

Abner was a relative of King Saul.

He was also captain of Saul's army and responsible for protecting the king. After Saul died and his son Ishbosheth became king, Abner supported Ishbosheth. He tried to get all the tribes of Israel to support the new king. But Abner could see that Ishbosheth was weak. Abner defected to David and promised to support him as king. David welcomed Abner's support. But Joab held a grudge against Abner for killing his brother Asahel years before. So Joab tricked Abner and killed him without David's knowledge. David was angry and sad. David called Abner a "great man."

See Abner's story in 1 Samuel 14:50–31:13; 2 Samuel 1:1–4:12; and 1 Kings 2:5, 32.

Key event
Reigns of Saul and David

Abraham (ay-bruh-ham)

Abraham was the father of the Jewish nation. He left his home in

Ur of the Chaldeans to find the land that God promised him. Most of his life he lived in Canaan as a wealthy owner of sheep, goats, and camels. At least two times Abraham saved his nephew Lot from serious injury or death. Once he rescued Lot from soldiers who had captured him.

Another time Abraham asked the Lord not to destroy the city of Sodom where Lot lived. The Lord destroyed the city, but he saved Lot first.

Abraham was very old when the son God had promised was born to him and Sarah. God also promised to bless all the nations through Abraham and Sarah's son, Isaac. Sometimes Abraham became impatient and tried to make God's promises come true by his own efforts. But in the end, "Abraham believed God, so God declared him to be righteous" (Romans 4:3).

See Abraham's story in Genesis 11-25; Acts 7:2-8; and Galatians 4:21-31. He is also celebrated in Hebrews 11:8-19.

Key Event

Time of the patriarchs; time of Abraham; destruction of Sodom and Gomorrah; time of Isaac

Relatives

Father: Terah
Wife: Sarah
Nephew: Lot
Sons: Ishmael and Isaac

Study Questions

• How many descendants did God promise Abraham? (Genesis 15:5-6)
• Why did God change Abraham's name? (Genesis 17:3-7)
• How did God test Abraham's love for him? (Genesis 22:1-13)

Absalom (ab-suh-luhm)

Absalom was one of King David's sons. He was a very handsome prince who was known for his beautiful long hair. But Absalom killed one of his half-brothers for raping his sister, Tamar. Then he ran away. King David mourned for his dead son, but he also missed Absalom.

Finally the king allowed Absalom to return. Later, Absalom rebelled against his father and tried to become king in David's place. He spoke kindly to the people and and won them over as friends. He persuaded many of them to follow him instead of King David. But in the end the king's loyal people defeated and killed Absalom.

See 2 Samuel 3:3 for a list of Absalom's brothers, and 2 Samuel 13–19 for the story of Absalom's life and death.

Key event
Rebellion against King David

Relatives
Father: David
Mother: Maacah
Brothers: Amnon, Kileab, Solomon, and others
Sister: Tamar

Study Questions
• How did handsome, proud Absalom die? (2 Samuel 18:9-18)
• How did King David react to Absalom's death? (2 Samuel 18:19-33)

Achan (ay-kuhn)

Achan was an Israelite when the people were entering the Promised Land. Achan disobeyed God's orders not to take anything from the city of Jericho. He took a beautiful robe, some silver, and a wedge of gold. He didn't think it would matter. But instead of an easy victory over the next city, the Israelites were defeated and several were killed. The Israelites were shocked and discouraged. God told Joshua that Achan had disobeyed and would have to be punished. Achan, his family, his belongings, and the stolen items had to be stoned and then burned. The place where all this happened was called the Valley of Achor, or "trouble," from that day on.

See Achan's story in Joshua 7:1-26; 22:20; 1 Chronicles 2:7.

Key event
Fall of Jericho

Adam and Eve (ad-uhm and eev)

Adam and Eve were the very first people. God created them in his image and they were his friends.

Adam named the animals. He and Eve cared for the animals and the Garden of Eden where they lived. Since there was no sin there, work was enjoyable. Adam and Eve had everything they needed to be happy with each other and with God. But Eve listened to Satan's lies that God was keeping something good from her and Adam. God told them not to eat the fruit from the tree of the knowledge of good and evil. Satan said if they would eat that fruit, they would become like God. Eve believed Satan. Sad to say, Adam also chose Satan's lies over God's truth. Instead of admitting that they had disobeyed God, they blamed each other.

See Genesis 1:26–5:5 for the creation and lives of Adam and Eve. Also read 1 Corinthians 15:22, 45 and 1

Timothy 2:13-14 to see what the apostle Paul said about
Adam and Eve.

Key event
Creation

Relatives
Children: Cain, Abel, Seth, and many others

Study Questions
• What did Adam and Eve do to hide their disobedience?
(Genesis 3:7-13)
• What were some results of Adam and Eve's sin?
(Genesis 3:14-24)

Adonijah (ad-uh-nye-juh)

Adonijah was King David's oldest living son when David was old.
It seemed he should be the next king. Many people followed
him, including Joab, one of David's officers. Adonijah planned his
own coronation. But he did not invite his brother Solomon or
others close to King David. When David heard Adonijah's plans,
he made Solomon king. Adonijah then feared for his life and
begged for mercy. Solomon said if Adonijah was loyal to him, he
would be safe. But Adonijah tried another way to become king.
He asked for one of King David's concubines. That would have
made him powerful. King Solomon became very angry and had
Adonijah killed.

See Adonijah's story in 1 Kings 1–2.

Key event
Reign and death of David

Agabus (ag-uh-buhss)

Agabus was one of the few prophets named in the New Testament. Prophets helped people understand God's will and encouraged them to obey. Agabus told about a very bad famine that was coming. The Christians were able to help others during

that hard time. Later Agabus predicted Paul's imprisonment. He acted this out by taking Paul's belt. He tied up his own hands and feet. He said the Jews would hand Paul over to the Gentiles. Paul's friends cried. They didn't want him to go to Jerusalem. But Paul asked them not to cry. He said he was ready to die for Jesus. God used Agabus to prepare Paul for what would happen.

See Agabus' story in Acts 11:25-30; 21:10-17.

Key event

Early church; Paul's third missionary journey

Ahab (ay-hab)

Ahab was the seventh king of Israel. He was also the most wicked king of Israel. He married Jezebel, who brought her god Baal for the people to worship. Ahab followed his wicked wife. The prophet Elijah tried to warn Ahab to stop sinning against the Lord. But Ahab didn't take his advice. Instead he got angry at

Elijah. Ahab pouted when he couldn't have some land he wanted. Jezebel wrongly accused the owner and had him killed. God sent Elijah to speak judgment on Jezebel and Ahab. At last Ahab humbled himself before the Lord. Then God lessened his punishment. **See Ahab's story in 1 Kings 16:28–22:40 and 2 Chronicles 18–22. In Micah 6:16, Israel is warned for following Ahab's ways.**

Key event
Ahab's rule

Ahasuerus
(ah-hah-zhoo-air-uhss)

Ahasuerus was also known as Xerxes I. He was the king of Persia when the Jews were in exile. He was very rich and ruled over 127 provinces from India to northern Egypt. Ahasuerus was a proud man. He became very angry when Queen Vashti refused to show off her beauty to the men at his banquet. He took away her status as queen. Then he made all the beautiful young women in the land become part of his harem till he found a new queen. He chose Esther, a Jewish girl whom God used to save her people.
See Ahasuerus' story in the book of Esther.

Key event
Captivity in Babylonia; time of Esther

Ahijah (uh-**hye**-juh)

Ahijah was a prophet from Shiloh during King Solomon's reign. Ahijah spoke against Solomon's idolatry. God used Ahijah to predict that the kingdom would be divided. A young man named Jeroboam would be one of the new rulers.

Here's how Ahijah told about it. Jeroboam was a good worker under King Solomon. Solomon gave him more responsibility and honor. One day the prophet Ahijah showed Jeroboam how God would divide the kingdom. Ahijah had on a new cloak. He tore it into 12 pieces and gave 10 of the pieces to Jeroboam. Ahijah told Jeroboam to be faithful to God like David had been. Then God would bless Jeroboam. But Jeroboam did not listen to

Ahijah. Years later, Ahijah told Jeroboam that God was destroying his family because of his wickedness. **See Ahijah's story in 1 Kings 11:26–40; 14:1-18.**

Key event
Reign of Solomon; kingdom divided; reigns of Jeroboam and
Rehoboam

Ahithophel (uh-**hith**-uh-fel)

Ahithophel was a special advisor to King David. The king would
ask him what he should do, and Ahithophel would give him
advice. David usually followed Ahithophel's suggestions because
"every word Ahithophel spoke seemed as wise as though it had
come directly from the mouth of God" (2 Samuel 16:23). Then
Absalom, the king's son, decided he wanted to become king. He
asked Ahithophel to help him. King David heard that Ahithophel
was helping Absalom. Then David asked God to make
Ahithophel's advice foolish. Absalom asked Ahithophel for advice
on attacking his father. Instead of listening to Ahithophel,
Absalom took another man's advice. This bothered Ahithophel
so much he went home and hanged himself!
See Ahithophel's story in 2 Samuel 15–17.

Key event
Absalom's rebellion; reign of David

Amaziah (am-uh-**zye**-uh)

Amaziah was Joash's son. Amaziah became king of Judah when he
was 25 years old. He did things that pleased the Lord, "but not
wholeheartedly" (2 Chronicles 25:2). He executed the people
who had killed his father. And he was careful not to punish the
children for their fathers' sins. He fought against the Edomites
and defeated them. But then he took their gods and worshiped
them—the very gods that were powerless to save the Edomites!

The Lord sent a prophet to warn Amaziah. But Amaziah was arrogant and said, "Since when have I asked your advice?" (2 Chronicles 25:16). Then Amaziah was defeated by the king of Israel. Later his own people murdered him.
See Amaziah's story in 2 Kings 14:1-23; 2 Chronicles 24:27–25:1-28.

Key event
Amaziah's reign

Amnon (am-non)

Amnon was King David's firstborn son and was heir to the throne. But Amnon didn't live long enough to become king. Amnon was spoiled. He had a half-sister named Tamar. Tamar was beautiful and Amnon desired her. But Amnon didn't ask the king to let him marry Tamar. Instead he pretended to be sick and asked her to come make him some food for him. Then he asked her to go to bed with him. When Tamar refused, Amnon raped her. What was worse, he then hated her and threw her out. King David did not punish his son. But Absalom took revenge and killed Amnon.

See Amnon's story in 2 Samuel 3:2; 13:1-39

Key event
King David's reign

Ananias and Sapphira
(an-uh-**nye**-uhss and suh-**fye**-ruh)

Ananias and Sapphira were a husband and wife couple who tried to deceive God. They belonged to the early church in Jerusalem. Ananias and Sapphira sold a piece of property. They pretended to give all the money to the apostles for the church. They kept some for themselves, but they told everyone that they had given all of it. They wanted people to think they were great. They could have kept it all or given as little or as much as they liked, just as long as they told the truth about it. But Peter knew they lied. He told Ananias he was lying to the Holy Spirit and Ananias fell down dead. Three hours later Sapphira also lied, and she died too! **See Ananias and Sapphira's story in Acts 5:1-11.**

Key event
Early church

Ananias (an-uh-**nye**-uhss)

Ananias was a faithful Jewish Christian in the city of Damascus when the apostle Paul became a Christian. Paul, known as Saul, was on his way to Damascus to arrest the followers of Jesus. Instead, the resurrected Jesus stopped him and changed his attitude. A bright light blinded Saul. God told Ananias to find Saul and pray for him. Ananias was afraid at first. He reminded the Lord that Saul was persecuting Christians. God assured Ananias that Saul was now going to tell people about Jesus. Ananias obeyed the Lord and found Saul. Ananias called Saul "brother." He prayed for Saul to be able to see again. Then he baptized Saul, who later became a leader in the church and a famous missionary. **See the story of Ananias in Acts 9:10-19; 22:12-16.**

Key event
Conversion of Saul

Andrew (an-droo)

Andrew was the first person named in the New Testament as a follower of Jesus. He had been a disciple of John the Baptist. Then John pointed to Jesus as the Lamb of God. Andrew and another person followed Jesus and spent the day with him. Then Andrew went to Simon, his brother, and told him, "We have found the Messiah." The brothers left their fishing nets immediately when Jesus said, "Follow me." Along with Philip, Andrew took some Greek men to talk to Jesus. It was Andrew who brought the little boy's lunch to Jesus when thousands of people were hungry. **See Andrew's story in Matthew 4:18-20; Mark 1:16-18; John 1:35-44; 6:8-9; 12:21-22; Luke 6:13-16; and Acts 1:13.**

Key event
Jesus' ministry

Anna (an-uh)

Anna was the first woman to recognize Jesus as the Messiah. Her husband had died when they were married for only seven years. After that, the widowed woman lived in the Temple in Jerusalem.

She spent most of her time worshiping God, fasting, and praying. Mary and Joseph took the infant Jesus to the Temple to present him to the Lord when he was eight days old. By then Anna had been there many years waiting for Messiah to come. She was 84 years old. Anna thanked God and told everyone who was looking for the Savior that he had come.
See Anna's story in Luke 2:36-38.

Key Event
Jesus' childhood

Apollos (uh-**pahl**-uhss)

Apollos was a Christian speaker, leader, and teacher in the early church. He came from Alexandria, Egypt where he learned the Old Testament Scriptures. He was a godly Jew who knew about repentance and the kind of baptism that John the Baptist taught. He spoke boldly in the synagogue but he didn't know that Messiah had already come. Priscilla and Aquila heard him and invited him home to hear the rest of the truth about Jesus. Then he debated publicly, using Scriptures to prove that Jesus is the Christ. Some people in Corinth divided into groups that followed Apollos, Paul, and Peter. Paul wrote to them to follow only Jesus.

See Apollos' story in Acts 18:24-28; 19:1. Paul mentions him in 1 Corinthians 1:12; 3:4-6; 4:1, 6; 16:12; and Titus 3:13.

Key Event

Early church

Aquila and Priscilla (uh-**kwil**-uh and pri-**sil**-uh)

Aquila and Priscilla were Jewish Christians from Rome who taught many people about Christ. The Emperor Claudius made a law against Jews in Rome. Aquila and Priscilla fled to Corinth. There they met Paul. They were all tentmakers, so they worked together. Paul thought highly of them both. He often mentioned Priscilla first in his letters. They traveled with him to Ephesus where they met Apollos. Priscilla and Aquila used their home to teach Apollos the full gospel. Later back in Rome, a church met in their home. Paul said

they risked their lives for him. Aquila and Priscilla are never mentioned separately in the Bible.

See Aquila and Priscilla's story in Acts 18; Romans 16:3-5; 1 Corinthians 16:19; and 2 Timothy 4:19.

Key event

Early church; Paul's second missionary journey

Asa (ay-suh)

Asa was Judah's third king; he was King Solomon's great-grand-son. Asa ruled for 41 years. The first 10 years he looked to the Lord for guidance. He put an end to idolatry in Judah. He took away his grandmother Maacah's status as queen because she worshiped idols. When enemies came from Ethiopia, Asa was wise and asked God for help. God gave him peace. Later, he sent gifts of gold to a heathen king and asked the king for help. God's prophet Hanani told Asa he did a foolish thing. Asa was angry and put Hanani in prison. Even when Asa's feet became diseased, he didn't repent of this wrong. But that was not the way Asa usually did things, because "Asa remained faithful to the Lord throughout his life" 1 Kings 15:14).

See Asa's story in 1 Kings 15:8-24 and 2 Chronicles 14–16.

Key event

Kings of Judah

Athaliah (ath-uh-lye-uh)

Athaliah was the only queen of Judah who ruled and one of the wickedest people who ever lived. She was the daughter of Ahab and Jezebel, wicked rulers of Israel. Athaliah married Jehoram, king of Judah. She brought Baal worship to Judah. She influenced her son Ahaziah to do evil. When he was killed, Athaliah set out

to kill all of the royal family—all her children and grandchildren! She ruled as queen for six years. Athaliah didn't know that one of her grandsons, Joash, had been rescued and hidden away. When Joash was seven years old, the priests gathered the people and declared him king. Athaliah died violently like her mother.
See Athaliah's story in 2 Kings 8:25–11:20 and 2 Chronicles 24:7.

Key event
Jehoram's reign; Athaliah's reign; Joash's reign

Balaam (bay-luhm)

Balaam was an Israelite hired by Balak, king of Moab, to curse the Israelites. At first, Balaam said he couldn't speak against the Lord's

command. But Balaam agreed When Balak offered to pay him. Along the way his donkey balked. After several beatings, the donkey talked! The angel of the Lord stood in the way. The donkey was more obedient than the man.

Balaam still went to see Balak and tried to curse the Israelites. But God wouldn't let him. The curses turned into   blessings. Balaam still tried to get around it—he told the Moabites to tempt the Israelites to sin. He thought that would take God's blessing away.

See Balaam's story in Numbers 22–24; 31:7, 8, 16. See New Testament warnings in 2 Peter 2:15-16; Jude 11; and Revelation 2:14.

Key event
End of the Exodus (traveling through Moab)

Barabbas (buh-**rab**-uhss)

Barabbas was the criminal whom Pilate set free to please the Jews. Barabbas was a robber and was guilty of murder in a rebellion against Rome. But every year at Passover, it was Pilate's custom to set a criminal free. Pilate knew the Jewish leaders hated Jesus and wanted to get rid of him. Pilate believed Jesus was innocent. He thought the people would choose to free Jesus. The leaders stirred up the crowd and yelled for the release of Barabbas. Pilate didn't want a riot, so he gave in to the people. Barabbas was set free. The Bible does not say if Barabbas understood that Jesus is the Savior.

See Barabbas' story in Matthew 27:11-26; Mark 15:6-15; Luke 23:18-25; and John 18:39-40.

Key event
Death of Christ

Barak (bair-uhk)

Barak was the leader
of the Israelite army
who wouldn't go into
battle unless
Deborah went with
him. Deborah gave
him God's message
to gather men from
the tribes of Naphtali
and Zebulun. He was
to lead them against
King Jabin, a
Canaanite. Jabin had
900 iron chariots and

was very cruel to the Israelite people. The commander of Jabin's
army was Sisera. Barak said he would go fight Sisera only if
Deborah went, too. Deborah warned Barak that the honor of
defeating the Canaanites would not go to him. A woman would
get the credit. It happened just as Deborah predicted. A woman
named Jael killed Sisera.
See Barak's story in Judges 4–5.
Key event
Time of the Judges

Barnabas (bar-nuh-buhss)

Barnabas' real name was Joseph. But because he was always saying kind words to people, the apostles named him Barnabas. That
name means "son of encouragement." Barnabas became a

Christian soon after Jesus' death and resurrection. He sold a piece of property and gave the money to the apostles to help the other Christians in Jerusalem. He also helped the Christians to trust Saul (later called Paul).

Barnabas was a teacher. The Holy Spirit chose him along with Paul to take the good news about Jesus to people in other cities. At first, Barnabas didn't realize that non-Jewish people could also become Christians. Paul helped him understand. Another time, Barnabas and Paul disagreed about taking John Mark on a missionary trip. They went on separate journeys and actually doubled the missionary work. Later Paul agreed with Barnabas that John Mark was a good worker.

See Acts 4:36, 37; 9:27–15:39 for Barnabas' story. Also read 1 Corinthians 9:6 and Galatians 2:1, 9, 13 to see what Paul said about Barnabas.

Key event
Paul's first missionary journey

Relatives
Aunt: Mary
Cousin: John Mark

Study Question
• Why did Barnabas and Paul disagree about taking John Mark on a missionary trip? (Acts 15:36-40)

Bartimaeus (bar-ti-**may**-uhss)

Bartimaeus was a blind beggar whom Jesus healed in the city of Jericho. He and another blind man were sitting along the side of the road. Jesus, his disciples, and a crowd of people were walking along the road. Bartimaeus heard all the commotion. When he found out it was Jesus, he called to him. "Lord, Son of David, have mercy on me!" Jesus told him to come to him and asked what he wanted. Bartimaeus said, "I want to see!" Jesus touched his eyes and told him his faith had made him well. Instantly, Bartimaeus could see.

He followed Jesus and praised God as he went. The others praised God, too.
See Bartimaeus' story in Matthew 20:29-34; Mark 10:46-52; and Luke 18:35-43.

Key event
Jesus' ministry

Baruch (bah-**rook**)

Baruch was Jeremiah's friend and scribe. God spoke to Jeremiah, then Jeremiah dictated the words to Baruch. Baruch wrote the words of the Lord on a scroll. Very few people could read or write, so Baruch was very special. Jeremiah was not allowed to go to the temple. He asked Baruch to go and read the words of the Lord to the people.
The prophecy told what would happen to Jerusalem. Later Baruch had to hide with Jeremiah. They were also both taken away to Egypt. Baruch worried about what was going to happen to him. God gave Jeremiah a special message for Baruch: "I will protect you wherever you go" (Jeremiah 45:5).

See Baruch's story in Jeremiah 32:6-16; 36:1-32; 43:1-7.

Key event

Jeremiah's prophecies; reigns of Zedekiah and Jehoiakim

Barzillai (bar-zil-eye)

Barzillai was a wealthy man from Gilead who helped King David when Absalom rebelled. King David and his family and supporters were fleeing from Jerusalem. Barzillai and some other men brought the king and his people food and bedding. Later when David was returning to Jerusalem he wanted Barzillai to go with him. But Barzillai was already 80 years old. He asked if he could

stay in his own hometown. So the king said good-bye to Barzillai and let him go home. When David instructed Solomon about the kingdom, he told him to be kind to Barzillai's family and let them eat at the king's table. **See Barzillai's story in 2 Samuel 17:27-29; 19:31-39; and 1 Kings 2:7.**

Key event

Absalom's rebellion; reign of David

Bathsheba (bath-**shee**-buh)

Bathsheba was the wife of King David and the mother of Solomon. Before she married David, though, she was the wife of Uriah, one of King David's mighty men. King David saw beautiful Bathsheba and sent for her to come to the palace. Was Bathsheba afraid to disobey the king, or glad the king wanted to see her? The Bible doesn't say what Bathsheba thought or felt. King David was already married and so was Bathsheba. But that night they slept together as if they were married to each other. Then Bathsheba went home. Bathsheba found out that she was pregnant and she told the king. In order to cover his sin, the king had Uriah killed. Then David married Bathsheba. God was very displeased. The baby that was born to Bathsheba and King David

got sick and died. Bathsheba disobeyed God, her husband died and then her baby died. Later, when King David repented, God gave him and Bathsheba another son. His name was Solomon. He became Israel's wisest king.

See Bathsheba's story in 2 Samuel 11–12 and 1 Kings 1–2.

Key event
Reign of David

Relatives
Father: Elim
First Husband: Uriah
Second Husband: David
Son: Solomon

Study Question
• How did Bathsheba make sure Solomon became king? (1 Kings 1:11-31)

Belshazzar
(**bel**-shuh-zar)

Belshazzar was the ruler of Babylon who saw a hand writing on the wall during a wild party. Belshazzar was ruling together with Nabonidus, his father. Belshazzar knew about King

Nebuchadnezzar's pride and how God had humbled him. But Belshazzar didn't respect the Lord. Instead he used the special gold goblets from God's temple for wine for his party. He and his guests were drinking and praising false gods. Suddenly he saw a hand writing words on the wall. No one knew what they meant. So they brought old Daniel in and asked him about it. He said they were a message from God. The message was that the kingdom would be given to the Medes and Persians. That night Belshazzar was killed by Darius the Mede.

See Belshazzar's story in Daniel 5.

Key event
Fall of Babylon

Benaiah (ben-eye-uh)

Benaiah was King David's captain of the bodyguard. He was a loyal, valiant man who stayed with David all through his battles and reign. Benaiah's father was Jehoiada the priest. Benaiah was a mighty man over the special group called the Thirty. He had 24,000 men in his division. When King David was ready to have Solomon become king, he told Benaiah to escort Solomon to Gihon to be anointed by the priests. Then Benaiah helped establish King Solomon's kingdom by getting rid of those who had been disloyal to David.

See Benaiah's story in 2 Samuel 23:20-23; 1 Kings 1:32-40; 2:28-35; 1 Chronicles 27:5-6.

Key event
Reigns of David and Solomon

Benjamin (ben-juh-min)

Benjamin was the youngest son of Jacob and Rachel and younger brother to Joseph. His mother died after giving birth to him and she named him Ben-oni, "Son of my sorrow." But Jacob changed his name to Benjamin, "Son of my right hand." After Jacob thought Joseph had been killed by a wild animal, Benjamin became his favorite son. When there was famine in Canaan, Jacob sent his sons

to Egypt to buy food. But he kept Benjamin at home with him. Joseph, who was ruler of Egypt, tested his brothers' love for their father and youngest brother to see if their attitude had changed. When Joseph finally told his brothers who he was, Benjamin was the first one he hugged and kissed.

See Benjamin's story in Genesis 35:16–49:28.

Key event

Time of the patriarchs; time of Jacob; time of Joseph's rule in Egypt

Bernice (bur-neess)

Bernice was a member of Roman royalty who heard the apostle Paul's defense of Christianity. She was the eldest daughter of Herod Agrippa I, the king of Judea. She was married to Herod Chalcis. Paul was on trial before Festus because the Jewish leaders didn't want him to preach about Jesus. Bernice and her brother King Agrippa II were visiting Festus. They wanted to hear Paul's story. Paul explained that Jesus was the fulfillment of Old Testament prophecies. Paul wanted Bernice and Agrippa to become Christians. But Bernice and the others didn't accept the good news about Jesus. Bernice lived an immoral

life even after this chance to have God change her heart.
See Bernice's story in Acts 25:13–26:32.

Key event
Paul's journey to Rome

Bezalel (bez-uh-lel)

Bezalel was an Israelite chosen by God to make beautiful things for the tabernacle during the Exodus. Bezalel knew how to work in gold, silver, bronze, gem stones, wood, and all kinds of crafts. God gave him a helper named Oholiab. These two men also were good teachers. They taught other people who wanted to

help with the fixtures and furnishings of the tabernacle. Many women spun yarn from wool, linen, and goat hair to make the cloth. The people freely brought their gold, silver, and other valuables for Bezalel and Oholiab's use. Bezalel and other skilled people made the beautiful items as God directed.

See Bezalel's story in Exodus 31:1-11; 35:4–6:3.

Key event

Making the tabernacle; the Exodus

Bildad (bil-dad)

Bildad was one of Job's friends who went to comfort him when he lost his family, his wealth, and health. The other two friends were Eliphaz and Zophar. They all agreed to visit Job in his time of sorrow. At first Bildad and the others sat quietly and just kept Job company. That was a good idea. But later they started giving advice and blaming Job for his troubles. Bildad said that Job and his children must have sinned and that God was punishing him. Job insisted he was innocent. God never explained to Job why he was suffering. But God did say that Bildad and the others were not speaking the truth about God.

See Bildad's speeches in Job 8, 18, and 25.

Key event
Suffering of Job

Boaz (boh-az)

Boaz was a rich farmer in Bethlehem who became the great-grandfather of King David. Boaz was related to Naomi, a widow who came back from Moab after a famine. Her husband and two sons had died in Moab. Naomi returned to Bethlehem with Ruth, one of her daughters-in-law. In Old Testament times, widows had very few rights. But a close relative, or kinsman-redeemer, could marry the widow so her husband's inheritance would not be lost. Boaz saw how kind Ruth, a young widow, was to Naomi, her mother-in-law. He married Ruth and they took care of Naomi. Boaz and Ruth had a son named Obed, who became King David's grandfather.

See Boaz' story in the book of Ruth.

Key event

The time of the judges

Caiaphas (kye-uh-fuhss)

Caiaphas was the high priest during the time of Jesus. As high priest, Caiaphas was leader of the Sanhedrin. The Sanhedrin was made up of the chief religious and legal leaders of the Jews. It was located in Jerusalem. Caiaphas was set up as high priest by the Romans. He was afraid Jesus was going to cause trouble and the Romans would take away Caiaphas' power. He said, "Why should the whole nation be destroyed? Let this one man die for the people." Caiaphas

didn't know he was predicting that Jesus would die for all people. He used his power to put Jesus on trial, find him guilty, and crucify him. He also tried to cover up the fact that Jesus rose from the dead. Later, he persecuted Stephen, Peter, and John.

See Matthew 26:3 and John 11:49-53 for Caiaphas' plot against Jesus. See Matthew 26:57-68 and John 18:12-28 for the illegal trial. See Acts 4:6 and 7:1 for persecution of Jesus' followers by Caiaphas.

Key event

Jesus crucifixion; the early church

Relatives
Father-in-law: Annas (who was high priest before him)
Study Question
• Why didn't Caiaphas and the other Jewish leaders kill Jesus themselves? (John 18:28-35)

Cain (kane)

Cain was the very first person born. His parents were Adam and Eve. Abel and Seth and many unnamed brothers and sisters were his family. They were born outside the Garden of Eden, after their parents disobeyed God. Cain was a farmer and he made an offering to God of crops instead of an animal offering. Cain became furious with Abel because Abel's offering was acceptable to God. God warned Cain that sin was going to destroy him. But Cain didn't listen to God. Instead he killed Abel. God put a mark on Cain so no one would hurt him. But then he sent him away. Cain wasn't sorry for his sin.

See Cain's story in Genesis 4:1-17 and 1 John 3:12.

Key event
Creation; outside the Garden

Caleb (kay-leb)

Caleb was one of the 12 spies who explored the land of Canaan after the Israelites left Egypt. Moses sent them out. They were gone 40 days and brought back samples of large fruit from the land. Caleb and Joshua were the only two spies who trusted that God would enable them to take the land. The other 10 men were afraid and said it would be too hard. Everyone grumbled. God said none of that generation except Caleb and Joshua would enter the

Promised Land. After wandering in the desert 40 years with the Israelites, Caleb was finally allowed to go in—when he was 85 years old! He fought the giants and God gave him victory.

See Caleb's story in Numbers 13–14, and Joshua 14–15.

Key event
The Exodus; entering the Promised Land

Cleopas (klee-oh-puhss)

Cleopas was one of two believers who met Jesus on the Road to Emmaus after Jesus' resurrection. They were walking the seven miles from Jerusalem to Emmaus. They talked about Jesus' death and the women's report that his body was not in the tomb. Jesus walked along with them, but they didn't recognize him. He asked what they were discussing. They were sad because they thought Jesus was going to set them free from Roman rule. Jesus explained all the Scriptures about himself and then started to leave. They invited him home with them. When Jesus sat down to eat with them, they suddenly realized who he was. Then he disappeared. Cleopas and his friend hurried back to Jerusalem to tell the others.

See Cleopas' story in Luke 24:13-35.

Key event
Jesus' resurrection

Cornelius (kor-**neel**-yuhss)

Cornelius was the first Gentile (non-Jew) to believe in Jesus and receive the Holy Spirit. He was a Roman centurion in Caesarea

known for his generosity to the needy. Cornelius and his family were devout, and he prayed to God regularly. God gave Cornelius a vision to invite Peter to his house. God also gave Peter a vision telling him to go to Cornelius' house. Jews were not supposed to enter a Gentile's house. But Peter obeyed God's vision to him. Cornelius gathered his family and friends and Peter told them about Jesus. Cornelius and his family believed in Jesus and were baptized.

See Cornelius' story in Acts 10.

Key event

Gentiles believe

Damaris (duh-mair-uhss)

Damaris was a woman who lived in Athens, Greece soon after Jesus died and rose again. People would gather in a place called the Areopagus and talk about new ideas. The apostle Paul went there to tell people about Jesus. The Athenians had many gods. But Paul told them about the true God, the "Lord of heaven and earth" (Acts 17:24). When Paul spoke of Jesus being raised from the dead, many people laughed. Some said they would talk more later. But Damaris was one of the few people who believed.

See Damaris' story in Acts 17:22-34.

Key Event
Paul's second missionary journey

Daniel (dan-yuhl)

Daniel was a young Jewish man from the royal family in Judah. In 605 B.C. he and many other Jews were captured by King Nebuchadnezzar and taken to Babylon. There Daniel and other young men learned how to serve the king. Even though Babylonians worshiped idols, Daniel and his friends worshiped only the Lord. God gave them special knowledge. God also gave Daniel the ability to understand the meaning of dreams. When the king had a dream but forgot it, Daniel was able to tell him what the dream was and what it meant.

Some men became jealous of Daniel and tricked the king into making a law against prayer. They knew Daniel prayed every day. But Daniel did not let the law change his devotion to God. When the king found out that Daniel was praying, he was sorry about the law, but he could not change it. Daniel was put into a den with hungry lions. But God protected him.

Daniel served four kings—Nebuchadnezzar, Belshazzar, Darius, and Cyrus—for about 60 years.

See Daniel 1–12 for the life of the prophet Daniel.

Key event

Exile in Babylonia

Relatives

None mentioned

Study Questions

• How was Daniel able to tell the king his dream? (Daniel 2:24-30)

• Besides interpreting dreams, how else did Daniel serve God in the court of the king? (Daniel 5:1-7, 13-14, 25-30)

• Why was it good that Daniel kept on praying for wisdom and did not give up? (Daniel 10:12-14)

David (day-vid)

David was the greatest king in Israel's history, the youngest of
Jesse's eight sons. As a boy, he took care of his father's sheep
while his brothers fought in King Saul's army.
But it was David that God chose
as the next king. David was
brave and skillful and killed
bears and lions with his
sling. God used David's
skill to defeat the
giant Goliath, Israel's
enemy. He was also
a skillful player of
the harp, and often
played it for King
Saul.

As king, David
did make some bad
mistakes. He commit-
ted adultery with
Bathsheba, and had her
husband killed so he could
marry her. As a father, he did
not train his sons properly.

But even with these problems, David truly loved the Lord and
always asked him to forgive his sins. David wrote many songs
recorded as Psalms in the Old Testament. God described David
as "a man after my own heart" (Acts 13:22). God also promised

that David would always have someone from his family be king. David was even an ancestor of Jesus Christ.
See David's story in 1 Samuel 16–31; 2 Samuel 1–24; and 1 Kings 1–2. You'll also find David's name in Hebrews 11:32, the list of the faithful.

Key event
Saul's reign; David's reign

Relatives
Father: Jesse
Wives: Michal, Ahinoam, Abigail, Bathsheba, others
Sons: Amnon, Kileab, Absalom, Adonijah, Solomon others
Daughters: Tamar, others

Study Questions
• Why didn't David kill King Saul? (1 Samuel 24:1-20)
• Why was David not allowed to build a temple for God? (1 Kings 5:3-5)
• What was David's connection to Jesus? (Mark 12:35-37)

Deborah (deb-uh-ruh)

Deborah was the fourth and only female judge of Israel. Her husband was Lappidoth. Deborah judged Israel in Ephraim. She decided disputes while sitting under a palm tree named after her. After 20 years of harsh treatment by the

Canaanite king Jabin, the people of Israel asked God for help.
God told Deborah to tell General Barak to gather men and fight
Jabin's commander, Sisera. Barak wouldn't go unless Deborah
went with him. Deborah agreed to go. But she prophesied that a
woman would get the credit for defeating Sisera. Barak routed
the troops but a woman named Jael killed Sisera. Deborah sang a
song about the battle. Israel had 40 years of peace under
Deborah's rule.

See Deborah's story in Judges 4–5.

<u>*Key event*</u>

Time of the Judges

Delilah (duh-**lye**-luh)

Delilah was the beautiful
woman who found out
the secret of Samson's
strength and betrayed him.
Samson loved Delilah, but
she was a Philistine
woman. So, Philistine
leaders bribed Delilah to
find out Samson's secret.
She pretended to love
him. But she wanted to
know his secret so she
could turn him over to
the Philistines and get rich.
Samson should have left. He was foolish. Instead he played games
with Delilah and made up answers. Finally, she nagged him so

much that he gave in and told his secret. The Philistines over-powered him and made him a slave. This is the only time Delilah is mentioned in the Bible.

See Delilah's story in Judges 16.

Key event
Time of the Judges

Demas (dee-muhss)

Demas was a coworker of Paul who deserted him. Paul took the Good News of Christ to various cities. Demas traveled with him. Demas sent greetings in letters to the church in Colosse and to Philemon. But when Paul was arrested and put in prison in Rome, Demas left him. Paul could have used Demas' help. The Roman prisons were damp and dark. Paul wrote to Timothy and asked him to bring his cloak. But Demas loved "the things of this life" (2 Timothy 4:10). That means he wanted the riches and ease of life rather than the hardship of spreading the Good News. The Bible doesn't say if Demas ever changed his mind and turned back to God.

See Demas' story in Colossians 4:14; Philemon 24; and 2 Timothy 4:10.

Key event
Paul's journey to Rome; Paul's imprisonment

Demetrius
(duh-**mee**-tree-uhss)

Demetrius was a silversmith in Ephesus who made silver idols of the false god Artemis (also called Diana). He opposed Paul's

preaching. (Paul said that people should not worship idols.) Demetrius was worried that he would lose money if people started worshiping the true God and not idols of Artemis. To make Paul stop preaching, Demetrius started a riot of silversmiths. They didn't say they were afraid of losing their jobs. They said they were protecting Artemis. A city official quieted the mob. He said Paul hadn't done anything wrong. Then he told Demetrius to take his complaint to court.

See the story of Demetrius in Acts 19:23-41.

Key event
Paul's third missionary journey

Dinah (dye-nuh)

Dinah was the daughter of Jacob and Leah. She is the only daughter mentioned in that family. She had 12 brothers. Shechem, the son of Hamor the Hivite, raped Dinah. That was a terrible thing to do. But later he asked Jacob to let him marry her. Dinah's brothers Simeon and Levi pretended to agree to the marriage. But they took revenge by attacking the city and killing all the men. The brothers took all the wealth of the city and took Dinah back home. Jacob was shocked and angry when he heard what his sons had done. He denounced them on his death bed (Genesis 49:5-7). No one knows what happened to Dinah.

See Dinah's story in Genesis 34.

Key event
Time of the patriarchs; time of Isaac; Jacob's family living in Canaan

Diotrephes (dye-ah-truh-feez)

Diotrephes was a man in the early church who tried to control a local group of believers. John wrote to his friend Gaius and warned him not to follow Diotrephes. Diotrephes opposed the apostle John and other spiritual leaders. He spread lies about them. Diotrephes would not help the Christians when they traveled from place to place to share the Good News of Christ. Whenever anyone helped the mission-aries, Diotrephes stopped them and put them out of the church. Diotrephes liked to be first and have power. **See the description of Diotrephes in 3 John 9-11.**

Key event
Early Church

Doeg (doh-eg)

Doeg was King Saul's chief shepherd and the man responsible for carrying out Saul's order to kill the priests of Nob. Doeg had seen David talking to Ahimelech the priest and assumed

Ahimelech was helping David against Saul. Actually, Ahimelech did not know that David was fleeing from Saul and was not guilty of betraying him. But Saul believed Doeg's lie and commanded his guards to kill Ahimelech, all the priests, and their families. The guards disobeyed Saul's orders and refused to kill the priests of the Lord. But Doeg did not hesitate. He killed 85 priests and their wives, children, infants, and animals. Only Abiathar escaped and told David. David said he should have known that Doeg would bring trouble. David accepted responsibility for the deaths. **See Doeg's story in 1 Samuel 21–22.**

Key event
Reign of Saul; David's flight from Saul

Dorcas (dor-kuhss)

Dorcas, or Tabitha, was a Christian woman who cared for the poor in the city of Joppa. Tabitha made clothes for the widows and their children and "was always doing kind things for others and helping the poor" (Acts 9:36). One day she became ill and died. Her friends were very sad. They tenderly prepared her body for burial. Peter was in Lydda. They sent for him and he went to the upstairs room where Tabitha's body was laid. The widows wept, telling all that Tabitha had done. Peter had everyone leave the room. Then he prayed, told her to get up, and she came back to life. Many people in Joppa believed in the Lord because of that miracle.

See Tabitha's story in Acts 9:36-42.

Key event
Early Church

Eleazar (el-ee-**ay**-zur)

Eleazar was the third son of Aaron; he became high priest when Aaron died. His brothers were Nadab, Abihu, and Ithamar. Their mother was Elisheba. His brothers Nadab and Abihu disobeyed the Lord in the way they offered the sacrifices, a sin that they paid for with their lives. When Aaron was old, God told Moses to make Eleazar high priest. Eleazar became adviser to Joshua when Moses died. And he was God's spokesman to the people. Eleazar helped Joshua take the people into the Promised Land. When Eleazar died, he was buried at Gibeah on land that had been given to his son Phinehas.

See Eleazar's story in Numbers 20:25-29; 27:15-23; Joshua 24:33.

Key event
Entering the Promised Land

Eli (ee-**lye**)

Eli was the high priest at Shiloh when Hannah went there and prayed for a son. Eli was high priest and judge of Israel for 40 years. He trained Samuel, the boy whom God gave to Hannah, to be a priest. Eli had two sons named Hophni and Phinehas. His sons were priests but they were immoral and disrespectful toward their duties. Eli told them they should not set such awful examples, but they did not obey him. Eli should have taken away their priesthood and punished them, but he did not. God said he would judge Eli, his sons, and his descendants. Eli, his sons, and Phinehas' wife all died in the same day.

See Eli's story in 1 Samuel 1–4 and 1 Kings 2:26-27.

Key event

Key event
Time of the judges; Ark of the Covenant captured

Eliezer (el-i-**ee**-zur)

Eliezer was Abraham's friend and steward who found a wife for Isaac. Sarah had died and Abraham wanted Isaac to marry before he died, too. He sent Eliezer back to Abraham's home country to find a wife for Isaac. Abraham didn't want Isaac to marry a woman from Canaan, because the women of Canaan worshiped idols. Eliezer asked God to help him find the right woman for Isaac. He loaded ten camels with gifts from Abraham and he and his men set out.

Eliezer spoke with a young woman at the well. She was Rebekah, from Abraham's family. Rebekah and her family agreed she would return with Eliezer and be Isaac's wife. Eliezer thanked God for guiding him.
See Eliezer's story in Genesis 24.

Key event
Time of the patriarchs; time of Abraham; time of Isaac; time of Jacob

65

Elijah (ee-**lye**-juh)

Elijah was Israel's most famous prophet besides Moses. God used him to speak to wicked King Ahab and Queen Jezebel. They led their people in worshiping the idol Baal. Elijah was involved in many miracles. He told Ahab that it wouldn't rain till he, Elijah, said it would. During the drought, God use ravens to feed Elijah. They brought him bread and meat. Later God kept a widow's oil and flour from running out so she, her son, and Elijah could eat.

One day the boy became ill and died. Elijah prayed for him three times and the boy's life returned. Elijah challenged the prophets of Baal and proved that the Lord is the true God. Though God used Elijah in many ways to

show God's power, Elijah sometimes became discouraged. At the end of his life, God took Elijah directly to heaven in a whirlwind. **See 1 Kings 17:1–22:53 and 2 Kings 1:1–2:11 for Elijah's story. Read about Elijah in the New Testament in Matthew 11:11-14 and James 5:16-18.**

Key event
Reign of Ahab

Relatives
None mentioned

Study Questions
• Why was Elijah afraid of Queen Jezebel? (1 Kings 19:1-5)
• At what special event did Elijah appear with Jesus? (Matthew 17:1-3)

Elisha (ee-lye-shuh)

Elisha was a prophet and friend of the prophet Elijah. Elisha succeeded Elijah as an important prophet in Israel for more than 50 years. (Prophets spoke to the people for God, helping them understand how to live.) Elisha often helped people. He helped a widow so her sons would not be taken away. He prayed for a dead boy and God brought him back to life. Once he even helped a commander of an enemy army be healed from leprosy.

God also gave Elisha special knowledge. Elisha was able to tell the king of Israel the secret plans of the king of Aram. The king of Aram thought there was a spy among his people. Instead it was God who revealed the secrets to Elisha. God also showed Elisha the army of heaven that was protecting him from the army of the king of Aram.

See 1 Kings 19:16–22:53 and 2 Kings 1:1–13:20 for the life of Elisha. See Luke 4:27 for the name of the man healed of leprosy.

Key event
Reigns of Jehu and Jehoahaz; life of Elijah

Relatives
Father: Shaphat

Study Questions
• What happened to the king's officer who doubted that God could save Samaria from famine? (2 Kings 7:1-20)

• How did God use Elisha to help someone even after Elisha had died? (2 Kings 13:20-21)

Elizabeth (e-liz-uh-beth)

Elizabeth was a godly woman who became the mother of John the Baptist. Zechariah, her husband, was a priest. Elizabeth and Zechariah were old and had no children. An angel announced to Zechariah that they would have a son. Zechariah had a hard time

believing this. But Elizabeth praised the Lord and thanked him. She believed what the angel said.

Elizabeth and Mary, Jesus' mother, were relatives. Mary visited Elizabeth when they were both pregnant. The baby in Elizabeth's womb leaped for joy and Elizabeth was filled with the Holy Spirit. Elizabeth was the first woman after Mary to know about the coming of the Savior. Her son would be the one to prepare the way for Messiah.

See Elizabeth's story in Luke 1:5-80.

Key event
Coming of Messiah (time of Jesus' birth)

Elymas (el-i-muhss)

Elymas was a sorcerer and false prophet who spoke against the apostle Paul's message about Christ. Elymas' Jewish name was Bar-Jesus, which means that his father was named Jesus. Elymas was an assistant to Sergius Paulus, the Roman ruler in the city of Paphos on the island of Cyprus. Sergius wanted to hear Paul and Barnabas explain the word of God. But Elymas didn't want him to believe and tried to deceive him. Finally Paul said Elymas was a child of the devil and would be blind for awhile. It happened just as Paul said. Elymas could not see and tried to find someone to lead him around. The Roman ruler believed the message about Christ.

See the story of Elymas in Acts 13:6-12.

Key event
Paul's first missionary journey

Enoch (ee-nok)

Enoch was a godly man who lived before the Flood. Enoch was the father of Methuselah and other sons and daughters. His father was named Jared. Enoch loved God and had a close friendship with him. He spoke to those around him about the Lord's coming to judge unbelievers. Enoch lived for 365 years. But he did not die. God just took him to Heaven. (Elijah was the other Old Testament person God took that way.) Enoch pleased God with his faith.

See Enoch's story in Genesis 5:18-24; Hebrews 11:5; and Jude 14–15.

Key event
Pre-flood patriarchs; the Flood; time of Abraham

Epaphras (ep-uh-frass)

Epaphras was the founder of the church at Colosse. He probably became a Christian in Ephesus when Paul was teaching and preaching there. Epaphras loved the believers and prayed diligently for them. Paul called him his "fellow prisoner in Christ" (Philemon 23). Epaphras went to Rome when Paul was there. He told Paul the problems the church was having. Some people were teaching false ideas about Jesus and the Christian life. Paul wrote the letter to the Colossians to make things clear. When Paul wrote the letter to Philemon, he sent greetings from Epaphras. The church of Colosse met in Philemon's home.

See Paul's words about Epaphras in Colossians 4:12 and Philemon 23.

Key event
The early Church; Paul's second missionary journey; Paul's third missionary journey; Paul's imprisonment in Rome

Epaphroditus (ee-**paf**-roh-**dye**-tuhss)

Epaphroditus was the messenger sent by the church of Philippi to help the apostle Paul. Epaphroditus delivered money that the church sent to support Paul in his ministry. He became ill and almost died. The people at Philippi were sad to hear that. And that made Epaphroditus sorry for them. God healed Epaphroditus and Paul said that was God's mercy to both of them. Paul called Epaphroditus a "true brother, a faithful worker, and a courageous soldier" (Philippians 2:25). Paul sent him back

to the church at Philippi and told the people to give him a warm welcome and to honor him and others like him. **See Paul's words about Epaphroditus in Philippians 2:25-30 and 4:14-19.**

Key event
The early Church; Paul's imprisonment in Rome

Esau (ee-saw)

Esau was a son of Isaac and Rebekah, and the twin brother of Jacob. Esau was red and hairy. He was also called "Edom" which means "red." He liked the outdoors and was a good archer. Esau was born right before Jacob and should have received the family birthright. That means he would get a double portion of inheritance from his father. It also meant he

would be the leader of the family when his father died. But Esau did things without thinking at a few important times. One day he came in from being outdoors while Jacob was making lentil stew. Esau demanded some, saying he was starving. Jacob bargained with Esau and said he'd give him stew if Esau would sell him the birthright. Esau thought only about how hungry he was and decided to sell his birthright to his brother. Later on, he regretted it.

See Genesis 25–36 for the whole story of Esau. See Hebrews 12:16-17 for a warning not to follow Esau's example.

Key event

Time of the patriarchs; time of Isaac; time of Jacob and Esau

Relatives

Grandparents: Abraham and Sarah

Parents: Isaac and Rebekah

Brother: Jacob

Wives: Judith, Basemathm, and Mahalath

Study Questions

• What did Esau do when he realized he didn't have the birthright or blessing? (Genesis 27:34-41)

• How did Jacob and Esau settle their dispute years later? (Genesis 33:1-20)

Esther (es-tur)

Esther was a young Jewish girl who lived in Persia at the end of the Israelites' exile there. Xerxes, king of Persia, wanted a new queen. He ordered all the beautiful young women to be taken to his palace. Esther was among them. In God's will and timing,

Esther was the one who pleased the king the most. Xerxes made Esther his new queen.

No one in the palace knew that Esther was Jewish, but it made a big difference that she was. The king's highest nobleman was Haman. Haman hated the Jews and made a plan to get rid of them all. Esther had a choice to make. Would she

let the king know she was Jewish, or would she be quiet and hope no one would find out? Esther chose to reveal her identity and expose Haman's plan. To do that she had to go to the throne room without being invited by the king. If he was angry, she would be put to death. God rewarded Esther's bravery and helped her save her people.

See the Book of Esther for Esther's story.

Key event
Jews taken to Babylon; Esther becomes queen

Relatives
Father: Abihail
Cousin: Mordecai
Husband: Xerxes

Study Questions
• Why did Haman want to kill the Jews? (Esther 3:1-6)
• How were the Jews rescued? (Esther 8:3-8; 9:1-10)

Eunice and Lois (yoo-niss and loh-iss)

Eunice and Lois were the mother and grandmother of Timothy, one of Paul's students. Eunice and Lois were Jewish Christians in the city of Lystra. They may have become believers during Paul's first missionary journey, when he was in Lystra (see Acts 14:6-18). Eunice's husband was a Greek and probably was not a believer. But Eunice and Lois taught Timothy about the Lord Jesus and he became a believer also. Paul recognized Eunice and Lois' faith as being passed on to their son and grandson, Timothy. **See the story of Eunice and Lois in Acts 16:1 and 2 Timothy 1:5.**

Key event
Paul's first missionary journey

Euodia and Syntyche (yoo-**oh**-dee-uh and **sin**-ti-**kee**)

Euodia and Syntyche were two Christian women in the church at Philippi. This church was formed during Paul's second missionary journey. It was the first church on the continent of Europe. Paul said that Euodia and Syntyche worked together with him to share the Good News. But they were having a problem getting along together. Their disagreement was public; other people knew about it. So Paul wrote about it briefly in the letter to the Philippian church. He asked Euodia and Syntyche, "Please,

because you belong to the Lord, settle your disagreement."
See the brief story in Philippians 4:2-3.

Key event
The early church; Paul's second missionary journey

Eutychus (yoo-tik-uhss)

Eutychus was a young man who fell out of a window one night when Paul was preaching. It was Paul's last night in Troas. He had a lot to say to his Christian friends. Eutychus was probably about 12 years old. He sat on the windowsill either to make room or to get some fresh air. But Paul preached till midnight and Eutychus fell asleep while he was listening. Worse yet, he fell out of the third story window and was killed! But Paul went down, put his arms around him, and Eutychus came back to life. Eutychus means "happy" or "fortunate." His family was certainly glad to have him alive.

See the story of Eutychus in Acts 20:7-12.

Key event
Paul's third missionary journey

Ezekiel (ee-zee-kee-uhl)

Ezekiel was a major prophet of Israel during the exile in Babylonia. He was training to be a priest in the Temple in Jerusalem when the Babylonians attacked Judah. They took

10,000 Jews captive. Ezekiel was among them. God changed Ezekiel's occupation to prophet to the captives in Babylonia. Other prophets about the same time were Daniel, Habakkuk, and Jeremiah. God gave Ezekiel exciting visions of what was going to happen to the

Israelites. Ezekiel acted out many of the prophecies God gave him. One time he lay on his side for 390 days. When his wife died, he was not allowed to mourn. These were directions that God gave Ezekiel. He obeyed, even though they were very difficult. Ezekiel was like a watchman on a city wall. He warned the people of the things that were coming.

See the book of Ezekiel and 2 Kings 24:10-17 for the things that happened to Israel and Ezekiel.

Key event
Jews taken captive to Babylonia

Relatives
Father: Buzi
Wife: unknown

Study Question
• What were God's instructions to Ezekiel about speaking to the Israelites? (Ezekiel 2:1-10)
• What was both good news and bad news about God's message to Ezekiel? (Ezekiel 33:10-20)

Ezra (ez-ruh)

Ezra was a Jewish priest and scribe who was in captivity in Persia during the reign of King Artaxerxes. Artaxerxes was the son of Xerxes, the husband of Queen Esther. Ezra was a man who "had determined to study and obey the law of the Lord and to teach. . . the people of Israel" (Ezra 7:10). Ezra asked the king for permission to return to Jerusalem. Artaxerxes let Ezra and 2,000 men and their families go and take whatever they needed for offerings to God.

The king sent Ezra as his delegate and told him to teach the Jews the Law of the Lord. Ezra and other leaders helped the people understand the ways they had sinned against God. They helped them repent and turn toward God.

See Ezra 7:1–10:16 for Ezra's story. See also Nehemiah 8:1–12:36 for more details from Nehemiah's point of view.

Key event
Jews returned to Jerusalem

Relatives
Father: Seriah

Study Questions
• What kinds of people went with Ezra to Jerusalem? (Ezra 7:7)
• Why did the king agree to let Ezra and so many people return to Jerusalem? (Ezra 7:27-28)

Felix (fee-liks)

Felix was the governor of Judea who kept Paul in prison in Caesarea. He was married to Drusilla, the daughter of King Herod Agrippa I. The Emperor Claudius appointed Felix to rule. But Emperor Nero recalled him to Rome because he was so cruel and greedy. Paul was on trial before Felix because the Jewish leaders wanted Paul executed. Paul defended himself. Felix called him a few days later to speak to him again. That time Paul talked about believing in Jesus Christ. Felix didn't like words about righteousness, self-control, and God's judgment. He sent Paul back to his cell. Felix hoped Paul would offer him a bribe, or money, to set him free.

See Felix's story in Acts 23:23–24:27.

Key event

Paul's journey to Rome

Gaius (gay-uhss)

There are two men named Gaius in the New Testament. This one was a friend of the apostle John. In fact, Gaius became a Christian because of John's work. John called him one of his children. Gaius used his home to offer hospitality to the Christians who traveled to spread the Good News. He gave them a place to stay and food to eat so they could continue their journey without worrying about having to pay for these things. John said Gaius was doing a good and important work. He said this was God's way of taking care

of the missionaries. Gaius was having a part in the work of telling the Good News by helping those who told it.

See John's words to Gaius in 3 John 1-8.

Key event
The early Church

Gamaliel (guh-may-lee-uhl)

Gamaliel was the most respected Jewish rabbi of the first century. He was a Pharisee and an expert in the Old Testament law. Saul of Tarsus, who later became the apostle Paul, studied under Gamaliel. Peter and the other apostles were preaching and healing people in Jesus' name. The high priest and his friends were jealous of the apostles' popularity. They arrested them and wanted to execute them. But Gamaliel said they should not fight against the apostles. He said if they were just a group of rebels, their cause would die out. But if they were God's messengers, they would succeed no matter what anyone did. Gamaliel advised the council to let them go.

See Gamaliel's story in Acts 5:33-42; 22:1-5.

Key event

Jesus' death and resurrection; early church

Gehazi (guh-**hay**-zee)

Gehazi was the servant of the prophet Elisha. He saw miracles that Elisha performed and heard the prophecies that God gave Elisha.

Gehazi was a useful helper and messenger, but he also brought great sorrow on himself for being greedy and deceitful. When Elisha healed Naaman's leprosy, Naaman wanted to pay the prophet. But Elisha refused the gifts of silver, gold, and fine clothes. After Naaman left, Gehazi followed him and said that Elisha had changed his mind. Gehazi was lying. Naaman gladly gave the things to Gehazi to take to Elisha. But Gehazi hid the things in his room. Elisha, being a prophet, knew

what happened. He said Gehazi and his descendants would have Naaman's leprosy forever. Gehazi immediately got leprosy. **See Gehazi's story in 2 Kings 4:11–8:6.**

Key event
Elisha's ministry

Gideon (gid-ee-uhn)

Gideon was a farmer and the fifth judge of Israel. Judges were people whom God used to lead Israel before they had kings. Judges helped the people obey God. At first Gideon was afraid. He destroyed an altar of the false god Baal. But he did it at night so no one would know he did it. Then God wanted Gideon to lead Israel against their enemies, the Midianites. Gideon asked for proof that God was with him. Finally Gideon believed God. Gideon called soldiers together. About 32,000 men came to fight. But God said there were too many. He told Gideon to send most of them home. God did not want the Israelites to think they had won on their own, without God's help. God helped Gideon and 300 men with swords, trumpets, and torches to surprise the Midianites and defeat them.

See Judges 6–8 for the life of Gideon. See Hebrews 11:32 where he's listed with other people of faith.

Key event
Time of the judges

Relatives
Father: Joash
Son: Abimelech, many others

Study Questions
• How long did Israel have peace because of Gideon? (Judges 8:28)
• What mistake did Gideon make after defeating the Midianites? (Judges 8:22–27)

Goliath (guh-**lye**-uhth)

Goliath was the Philistine giant from Gath who was killed by young David. Goliath was more than nine feet tall. For 40 days he taunted the army of Israel. He challenged Israel's best soldiers to fight him. Goliath wore a bronze helmet. His coat of armor weighed 125 pounds.

His leg coverings were also made of bronze. The point of his spear weighed 15 pounds. He had a man who carried his shield in front of him. Goliath was heavily protected, strong, and tall. The Israelites were all terrified of him. But young David was not afraid of him. He wore no armor and carried only a bag of five stones and his sling. But he trusted in the living God, and that made all the difference.

See Goliath's story in 1 Samuel 17.

Key event
Reign of Saul

Gomer (goh-mur)

Gomer was the wife of the prophet Hosea. She was an unfaithful wife who left Hosea for other men. She was sold into slavery. She had three children. God told Hosea to name them with sad names such as "Not Loved" and "Not My People." God told Hosea that these children and his wife were like his people, the Israelites. God had made them his special people. The people had promised to love and obey God. But over and over the Israelites looked for help from other countries. And over and over they worshiped idols. God told Hosea to take Gomer back and love her. God said this was a picture of how he loved his people, even though they did not love him.

See Gomer's story in Hosea 1–3.

Key event
Israel's captivity

Habakkuk (huh-**bak**-uhk)

Habakkuk was a prophet in Judah before the Babylonians captured Jerusalem. He lived during the reign of King Jehoiakim. The small book of Habakkuk was written by this prophet. Habakkuk saw all the wickedness of his people in Judah. He prayed to the Lord about all the evil. God told Habakkuk he would send punishment through the Babylonians. Habakkuk was troubled that God would use a nation even more wicked than Judah to punish his people. But God assured him that God is in control and will make everything right in the end. Habakkuk was given the reassuring words, "the righteous shall live by their faith" (Habakkuk 2:4).

See Habakkuk's prayer in the book of Habakkuk.

Key event

Jehoiakim's reign; time of the exile

Hagar (**hay**-gar)

Hagar was the Egyptian servant of Sarah who became the mother of Ishmael. Sarah was getting old and still did not have the son God had promised when she gave Hagar to Abraham as a substitute wife. Sarah thought it would be better for Abraham to have a son by another woman than to

wait for God to do a miracle. But Sarah was not trusting God's promise. This caused many problems. Hagar became pregnant and did have a son, but it was not the son of God's promise. And Hagar began to think she was better than Sarah. Then Sarah got jealous and treated Hagar harshly. Later, when Sarah's son Isaac was born, she sent Hagar and Ishmael away. But the Lord promised Hagar that her son would become a great nation. The Arab people are descended from Hagar and Ishmael. **See Hagar's story in Genesis 16:1-16 and 21:8-20.**

Key event

Time of the patriarchs; time of Abraham; birth of Isaac

Haggai (hag-eye)

Haggai was a prophet to the people of Jerusalem after they returned from their captivity in Babylonia. Haggai wrote the Old Testament book of Haggai. The people had been back for 20 years. But they had not worked on the Temple for about 15 years. Instead they built their own homes. They were living in nice comfortable homes while the Temple was a shambles.

God warned the people through Haggai that they were not doing what mattered most. They were neglecting their spiritual life. Haggai and the prophet Zechariah encouraged the people to rebuild the Temple and worship God. When they got serious, the people finished the Temple in a few years.

See Haggai's message in the book of Haggai. See how he helped in Ezra 5:1; 6:14.

Key event

Time of the exile; rebuilding of the Temple afterward

Haman (hay-min)

Haman was the favorite officer of King Xerxes of Persia during the time of Esther. The king had made Haman second only to himself. Haman was very proud. But a Jew named Mordecai refused to bow to Haman when he passed by. That made Haman furious. Haman's ancestors were Amalekites; Jews and Amalekites were longtime enemies. Haman's wife, Zeresh, and his friends said he was right to be so angry at Mordecai. So Haman made a plan to hang Mordecai and slaughter all the Jews

in the kingdom. But God had made the Jewish woman, Esther, the queen. She foiled Haman's plot. Haman was hanged on the gallows he had built for Mordecai.

See Haman's story in the book of Esther.

Key event
Time of the exile; time of Esther in Persia

Hanani (han-uh-**nye**)

Hanani was a prophet who spoke out against King Asa of Judah.
The king had trusted the Lord to give him and his army victory in
a battle against the Cushites. Then the king of Israel threatened
Judah. This time King Asa did not ask the Lord for help. Instead
he sent money to the king of Aram. The prophet Hanani told Asa
he had done a foolish thing. Hanani's message from God was that
Asa would be at war without God's help. King Asa became so
angry he put Hanani into prison.
See Hanani's story in 2 Chronicles 16:7-10.

Key event
Reigns of Abijah, Asa, and Jehoshaphat in the south; reign of
Jeroboam I in the north

Hananiah (han-uh-**nye**-uh)

Hananiah was a false prophet who spoke against the prophecy of
Jeremiah. Hananiah lived in Jerusalem during King Zedekiah's
reign. He told the priests and the people that God was going to
defeat the Babylonians. Hananiah's prophecy was popular
because he spoke of peace. It was the opposite of what God told
Jeremiah to tell the people. Jeremiah wore a wooden yoke as a
sign of the slavery Judah would be under in Babylonia. Hananiah
broke it and said the people would be free. God told Jeremiah to
tell the people they would be under an iron yoke. God also told
Jeremiah to tell Hananiah he would die within a year. He did!
See Hananiah's story in Jeremiah 28.

Key event
Captivity of Jerusalem; time of the exile; reign of Zedekiah

Hannah (han-uh)

Hannah was the mother of the prophet Samuel. Her husband was Elkanah. For many years Hannah could not have children. She was very sad. She asked God for a son. She promised God that if he gave her a son she would give him back to serve the

Lord. God granted Hannah's request. When Samuel was about three years old, Hannah took him to the Tabernacle. She left Samuel with the priest Eli. Every year she took a new robe to her son. Samuel grew up to become a great leader in Israel. Later Hannah had three other sons and two daughters. When Samuel was a prophet, he often lived in his mother's town. **See Hannah's story in 1 Samuel 1–2.**

Key event
Time of the Judges

Herod (hair-uhd)

There were several kings of the Jews named Herod. They lived from the time before Jesus was born till about 60 years after his death and resurrection. They all had opportunities to trust in God, but they all refused.

The first one was **Herod the Great**. The Magi visited him to ask about the new King of the Jews, Jesus. Herod the Great pretended to want to worship the baby. Instead, he ordered the death of all baby boys two years and younger in Bethlehem.

His son **Herod Antipas** ordered John the Baptist put into prison and later had him beheaded. He also had a part in Jesus' trial.

Herod Agrippa I persecuted the early Church. He ordered the murder of the apostle James. Then he imprisoned Peter and planned to have him executed. But an angel took Peter out of prison at night. This king also accepted the people's praise of him as a god. The Lord made him die soon after.

Herod Agrippa II listened to the apostle Paul's defense. He was amused that Paul wanted him to become a Christian.

See their stories in Matthew, Mark, Luke, John, and Acts.

Key event
Birth of Christ; death and resurrection of Christ; early church

Relatives
Herod the Great
Father: Antipater
Sons: Archelaus, Antipater, Herod Antipas, Philip, others
Wives: Doris, Mariamne, others
Herod Antipas
Father: Herod the Great
Mother: Malthace
Second wife: Herodias
Herod Agrippa I
Grandfather: Herod the Great
Father: Aristobulus
Uncle: Herod Antipas
Sister: Herodias
Wife: Cypros
Son: Herod Agrippa II
Daughters: Bernice, Mariamne, Drusilla
Herod Agrippa II
Great-grandfather: Herod the Great
Great uncle: Herod Antipas
Father: Herod Agrippa I
Sisters: Bernice, Mariamne, Drusilla

Study Questions
• What great event happened during the reign of Herod the
Great? (Matthew 2:1-12)
• What happened while Herod Antipas ruled over Galilee?
(Luke 3:1-3)

• How did Herod Agrippa I contribute to his own death? (Acts 12:20-23)

• What great opportunity did Herod Agrippa II miss? (Acts 26:1-32)

Herodias (huh-**roh**-dee-uhss)

Herodias was a granddaughter of Herod the Great and the woman who caused John the Baptist to be beheaded. (Herod the Great is the one who ordered the boy babies in Bethlehem to be killed when he learned of Jesus being born.) Herodias first was married to Herod Philip. Their daughter was Salome. But Herodias left Philip for Herod Antipas (the tetrarch). John the Baptist spoke against their sin. Herodias hated him for it. She made Herod have John arrested and wanted John killed. But Herod was afraid to hurt John because the people liked him. Herodias got her way when Salome danced at Herod's birthday party. Herod was so pleased he promised her anything she wanted. Salome asked her mother what to do. Herodias said, "Ask for John the Baptist's head."

See Herodias' story in Mark 6:16-29 and Matthew 14:1-12.

Key event

Ministry of Christ; death of John the Baptist

Hezekiah (hez-uh-**kye**-uh)

Hezekiah was a wise and godly king of Judah. His parents were Ahaz and Abijah. Hezekiah began reigning when he was 25 years old and reigned for 29 years. He trusted and followed the Lord. Hezekiah destroyed the pagan altars, idols, and temples in Judah. He opened the Temple of the Lord that his father had closed. He restored proper worship of God and made Passover a national holiday again. Hezekiah had several books of Proverbs copied and preserved. When an enemy king sent a letter threatening Judah, Hezekiah took the letter before the Lord and prayed for help. A foolish thing he did was to show off his wealth to foreign rulers. But because of his devotion to God, God gave Hezekiah a peaceful reign.

See Hezekiah's story in 2 Kings 16:20–20:21; 2 Chronicles 28:27–32:33; Isaiah 36:1–39:8.

Key event

Reigns of Ahaz, Hezekiah, and Manasseh

Hilkiah (hil-**kye**-uh)

Hilkiah was the high priest during the reign of King Josiah of Judah. While cleaning out the Temple for the king, Hilkiah found the Book of the Law (God's law). It had been missing for many years. Hilkiah told Shaphan the scribe what he found. Then Shaphan took it to King Josiah. This discovery resulted in one of the greatest times in Judah's history. All of the leaders and people made new commitments to love and obey God. At Josiah's command, Hilkiah and the other priests asked the prophetess Huldah what they should do. They removed all the items made to worship the false gods Baal, Ashereh, and the stars. Hilkiah lived to see the return of respect for the law and the Temple. **See Hilkiah's story in 2 Kings 22:1–23:24 and 2 Chronicles 34:1–35:19.**

Key event
Reigns of Amon, Josiah, and Jehoahaz

Hiram (hye-ruhm)

Hiram was the king of Tyre and a friend of King David and King Solomon. He supplied materials and workmen to David to build his palace. He did the same for Solomon during construction of the Temple. Hiram supplied all the cedar and pine logs that Solomon needed. In return, Solomon paid him with wheat and olive oil. Hiram must have been a believer in the Lord. In a letter to Solomon, he said,

"Blessed be the Lord, the God of Israel, who made the heavens and the earth!" (2 Chronicles 2:12).

See Hiram's story in 2 Samuel 5:11; 1 Kings 5:1-18; 2 Chronicles 2:3-16.

Key event
Reigns of David and Solomon; construction of Solomon's Temple

Hosea (hoh-**zay**-uh)

Hosea was a prophet of God to Israel. His name means "salvation." God wanted Hosea to show the people of Israel how much God loved them. He had Hosea marry a woman named Gomer who was an unfaithful wife. God said that Gomer was like Israel. She was not true to Hosea just as Israel was not true to God. Gomer and Hosea had a son. Then Gomer had two other children, but Hosea was not sure they were his. How sad Hosea was to have an unfaithful wife. Then God told Hosea to go and buy her back from slavery and to love

her. Hosea's love for Gomer showed God's forgiveness and love for his people.

See the book of Hosea.

Key event

Reigns of Uzziah, Ahaz, Jotham, and Hezekiah in the south; and Jeroboam II and Hoshea in the north

Huldah (huhl-duh)

Huldah was a prophetess who lived in Jerusalem in Judah during King Josiah's reign. Her husband was Shallum, the king's valet. The Jews had neglected the Temple and God's Word for many years. Josiah told the priests to repair the Temple. They found a scroll of the Book of the Law. Josiah was sorry to see how far from God his people were. He asked the priests to find out what they should do. The priests went to the prophetess, Huldah. She prophesied that God was going to send judgment on Judah for worshiping idols. But because Josiah was sorry for Israel's sin, God gave Josiah a time of peace.

See Huldah's story in 2 Kings 22:14-20 and 2 Chronicles 34:19-28.

Key event

Reign of Josiah

Hushai (hoo-shye)

Hushai was a friend of King David who pretended to support Absalom during Absalom's rebellion. David had left Jerusalem to get away from Absalom. Hushai was sad as David left and wanted to go with him. But David asked him to go to Jerusalem and pretend to be on Absalom's side. David wanted Hushai to give Absalom bad advice. The priests stayed in Jerusalem too and then Hushai passed messages to them. Their sons took the information to David. Ahithophel, another adviser, gave good advice. But God wanted Absalom to fail, so God made Hushai's bad advice sound good to Absalom.

See Hushai's story in 2 Samuel 15:32-37 and 16:15–17:16.

Key event
Reign of David; Absalom's rebellion

Isaac (eye-zik)

The name Isaac means "he laughs." It is the name that God gave to Abraham and Sarah's son Isaac, the son God had promised them. Isaac was born when Sarah was 90 years old and Abraham was 100. God said that he would bless the nations through Isaac.

God used Isaac to test Abraham's faith. He told Abraham to show how much he loved God by sacrificing his son Isaac. Just when Abraham was ready to kill Isaac, God stopped him. God provided a ram for the sacrifice.

Isaac grew up trusting God to keep his promises. He taught his sons to trust God, too. But sometimes he lied to get out of trouble. He found out that this only causes more problems. But God blessed Isaac and he became wealthy from his crops and animals. Many years later, Jesus was born as a descendent of this family.
See Isaac's story in Genesis 17:15–35:29. See Hebrews 11:17-20 to read about the faith in this family.

Key event
Time of the patriarchs; time of Abraham; time of Jacob

Relatives
Parents: Abraham and Sarah
Half brother: Ishmael
Wife: Rebekah
Sons: Jacob and Esau

Study Questions
• How did Rebekah become Isaac's wife? (Genesis 24:1-67)
• Why did Jacob trick Isaac? (Genesis 27:19)

Isaiah (eye-zay-uh)

Isaiah was one of the greatest Old Testament prophets. He prophesied during the reigns of four kings of Judah. He was also a scribe and he wrote the book of Isaiah. Isaiah saw the holiness of the Lord in the Temple. The prophet realized how sinful he and his people were. But God forgave him, and Isaiah volunteered to take God's message to the world. After that he was never the same. He preached about judgment and hope. God told Isaiah the people would not listen to him but to still warn them of judgment. Isaiah made many prophecies about the coming of the Messiah. At least 50 times Isaiah is quoted in the New Testament.

See Isaiah's story in Isaiah 6 and 2 Kings 19:2–20:19. Fulfilled prophecies are in Matthew 3:3 and Romans 10:16, 20-21.

Key event
Reigns of Jotham, Ahaz, Hezekiah, and Manasseh; Assyrian siege of Jerusalem

Ishbosheth (ish-boh-sheth)

Ishbosheth was a son of Saul who laid claim to the throne right after Saul died even though God had made David king. King Saul, Jonathan, and two other sons were all killed in battle on the same day. Abner, Saul's commander, said that Ishbosheth was the new king, but actually David was. Ishbosheth was 40 years old at the time and resisted David's forces for two years. When Abner was killed, Ishbosheth didn't have courage to keep trying. Two of his own officers killed him in his bed as he rested from the noon day heat. The officers thought they were doing King David a favor. But David had them executed for killing an "innocent man in his own house and on his own bed" (2 Samuel 4:11).

See Ishbosheth's story in 2 Samuel 2:8–4:12.

Key event
Reigns of Saul and David

Ishmael (ish-may-el)

Ishmael was the son of Abraham and Hagar. His name means "God hears." Abraham thought Ishmael was the son God had promised to him. But God's plan was for Abraham and Sarah to have a son. When Isaac was a young child, Ishmael made fun of him. Sarah got angry and insisted that Abraham send Hagar and Ishmael away. But God promised to bless Ishmael also. God took care of him in the desert. Ishmael became a good archer and hunter. He married and had 12 sons. Ishmael was not the one through whom Messiah would come. But God did bless him with a long life and many descendants—the Arab people.

See Ishmael's story in Genesis 16:1–17:27; 21:8-21; 25:12-18. He was not the promised son: Romans 9:7-9; Galatians 4:21-31.

Key event

Life of the patriarchs; time of Abraham; time of Jacob

Jacob (jay-kuhb)

Jacob was the younger twin of Esau. He tricked his brother into selling his birthright. Then he tricked his father into blessing him instead of his older brother. Jacob had to leave home because Esau wanted to kill him. Then the tricker was tricked by his uncle Laban. Jacob worked seven years for his bride. Jacob thought he was marrying Laban's daughter Rachel, but Laban let him marry her sister Leah instead! Jacob loved Rachel so much that he worked another seven years for her. Jacob became the father of the 12 tribes of Israel. He was a shepherd and his wealth came from his farm animals, like his father before him. Later he learned to depend on God, and God changed his name to Israel. **See Jacob's story in Genesis 25–50. See also Matthew 22:23; Romans 9:11-13; and Hebrews 11:9, 20–21 for God's descriptions of Jacob.**

Key event

Time of the patriarchs; time of Isaac; Jacob and his family move to Egypt

Relatives
Parents: Isaac and Rebekah
Brother: Esau
Uncle and father-in-law: Laban
Wives: Rachel and Leah
Children: Twelve sons (including Joseph) and one daughter are named in Bible

Study Questions
• How did Jacob deceive his father? (Genesis 27:1-30)
• What was the meeting like between Jacob and Esau after their terrible dispute over their father's blessing? (Genesis 33:1-17)
• How did Jacob describe God? (Genesis 48:15-16)

Jael (jay-el)

Jael was the woman who killed Sisera, commander of the Canaanite army during the time of Deborah. Jael's husband was Heber, the Kenite. Heber was friends with the Canaanites. But Jael was not. With God's help, Barak, the commander of the Israelites, defeated the Canaanite army. But Sisera ran away and Barak did not know where he was. Sisera thought he would be safe in Jael's tent. She gave him milk to drink and he fell asleep. While he was sleeping, she killed him with a tent peg. Barak came looking for Sisera and Jael showed him where he was. Jael received the honor for defeating the powerful Canaanite army commander—just as Deborah had prophesied.

See Jael's story in Judges 4–5.

Key event
Time of the Judges

Jairus (jye-ruhss)

Jairus was the synagogue ruler who asked Jesus to heal his dying daughter. Jairus was an elected official and had a lot of responsibility in his town. But he bowed before Jesus and showed him great respect. Jairus' daughter was about 12 years old. She was his only daughter and she was very ill. Before Jesus got to Jairus' house a messenger told them the girl had died. Jesus told Jairus not to give up hope but to believe. It took faith for Jairus to continue to believe that Jesus could heal his dead daughter. Jesus honored that faith and brought the girl back to life.

See Jairus' story in Mark 5:21-43 and Luke 8:41-56.

Key event
Jesus' ministry

James (jaymz) (Jesus' brother)

James did not believe Jesus was the Messiah at first. It was not until Jesus died on the cross and rose from the dead that James and Jesus' other brothers believed. Jesus' other brothers were named Joseph, Simon, and Jude. He had sisters, too. James later became the leader of the church in Jerusalem. He also wrote the letter of James in the New Testament. He wrote it to help Christians who were scattered throughout the Roman Empire. **See the story of James in Matthew 13:53-57; John 7:5; 1 Corinthians 15:7; Acts 1:14; 15:13; James 1:1.**

Key event

Jesus' ministry; Jerusalem Council (early church)

James (jaymz) (disciple of Christ)

James was one of Jesus' closest disciples. His parents were Zebedee and Salome and his younger brother was John. Zebedee, James, and John were fishermen. James, John, and Peter were Jesus' inner circle of followers. They were with Jesus when he raised Jairus' daughter from death, and they were at Jesus'

Transfiguration. Jesus called James and John "sons of thunder." Once when some people did not welcome Jesus, James and John wanted to call fire down on them. James and his brother also asked Jesus for special places in his kingdom. But after Jesus' death and resurrection, James realized Jesus' kingdom was in heaven, not on earth. James was the first apostle to die for his belief in Jesus.

See James' story in Matthew, Mark, Luke, and John, and in Acts 1:13; 12:1-3.

Key event

Jesus' ministry; early church

Jason (jay-suhn)

Jason was a believer who lived in Thessalonica and helped Paul and Silas. Jason opened his home so Paul and Silas had a place to stay in the city. Thessalonica was one of the wealthiest cities in Macedonia. Paul and Silas went to the synagogue and taught that Jesus fulfilled the Old Testament prophecies. Some Jews, Greeks, and leading women followed Paul and Silas. Then the Jewish leaders became jealous. They stirred up a riot and went to Jason's house to get Paul and Silas. But they were not there. The leaders pulled Jason and other believers out and took them to the officials. Jason had to pay money to be able to leave.

See Jason's story in Acts 17:1-9.

Key event

Paul's second missionary journey

Jeremiah (jer-uh-**mye**-uh)

Jeremiah was a prophet to the people of Judah. He tried to warn the people to repent of their sins and turn to God. God gave Jeremiah visions of the destruction that would come if people did not listen. But the people would not believe him, and this made Jeremiah very sad. Jeremiah is called the "weeping prophet." He wrote the book of Jeremiah to warn about Judah's capture. He wrote the book of Lamentations, looking back on the destruction of Jerusalem. Jeremiah saw other prophets murdered. He also

was persecuted for telling the people about their sin. One time some people put him down in an empty cistern, something like a well. It didn't have water in it but deep mud. Jeremiah sank down into the mud. Even though the people would not listen, Jeremiah did not give up.

See the book of Jeremiah for Jeremiah's story. See Ezra 1:1; Daniel 9:2; Matthew 2:17; 27:9-10 for some of Jeremiah's prophecies.

Key event
Reigns of Josiah and Zedekiah; destruction of Jerusalem

Relatives
Father: Hilkiah

Study Questions
• Why was Jeremiah put into a cistern and how did he get out? (Jeremiah 38:4-13)
• What did the Babylonians do when they captured Jerusalem? (Jeremiah 39:1-14)
• How was Jeremiah like Jesus? (Jeremiah 12:6; Matthew 13:57)

Jesse (jess-ee)

Jesse was David's father. He was a sheep herder in Bethlehem and a descendant of Ruth. The Lord told the prophet Samuel to go see Jesse. God had chosen one of Jesse's eight sons to be king after Saul. Samuel invited Jesse and his sons to worship the Lord with him. As each of Jesse's sons walked past, Samuel thought that one must be the chosen one. Eliab, Abinadab, Shammah, and

the next four sons each passed before Samuel. But God told him they were not his choice. Samuel asked Jesse if there were any more sons . Jesse sent for David. David was the son of Jesse the Lord had chosen.

See Jesse's story in 1 Samuel 16:1-13 and 17:25-58.

Key event

Reign of Saul; anointing of David; defeat of Goliath

Jethro (jeth-roh)

The man Jethro was also called Reuel, "friend of God." He was a shepherd and a priest to the Midianite people. That meant he worshiped false gods. But he was kind to guests. When Moses ran away from Pharaoh as a young man, Jethro invited him to stay with him. Later, Moses married Jethro's daughter, Zipporah. After many years, God told Moses to go talk to the king of Egypt about letting the Israelites leave Egypt. Jethro took care of Moses' wife and two sons while Moses led the people out. Then Jethro took Moses' family to him in the desert. It was a happy reunion. Jethro was glad to hear all that God had done for the people of Israel. He said, "I know now that the Lord is greater than all other gods" (Exodus 18:11). Jethro was also wise. Moses was working all day long as a judge. Jethro advised Moses to let other leaders help him settle disputes between the people. Moses gladly took his advice.

**See Exodus 2:15–3:1;
18:1-17 for Jethro's story.**

Key event
The Exodus

Relatives
Children: Seven daughters, including Zipporah, and one son, Hobab
Son-in-law: Moses

Study Question
• What plan did Jethro give Moses? (Exodus 18:17-26)

Jezebel (jez-uh-bel)

Jezebel was the queen of Israel in Samaria alongside her husband King Ahab. Jezebel was not from Israel and she did not trust in God. In fact, she hated God and worshiped the idols Baal and Asherah. She had 850 pagan priests for her false gods. Jezebel was a very powerful woman who used her power for evil. She led the people of Israel into idolatry. As a result, later God punished the people with captivity.

Jezebel is known as one of the most wicked women in the Bible. She persecuted the true prophets. She especially hated the prophet Elijah because he showed that the Lord is the true God. Jezebel was so bad that her name is used in the Book of Revelation as a symbol for evil.

See Jezebel's story in 1 Kings 16:31–22:53 and 2 Kings 1:1–9:37. See Revelation 2:20-21 for another woman called "Jezebel" because of her wickedness.

Key event
Reign of Ahab; time of Elijah

Relatives
Husband: Ahab
Father: Ethbaal
Sons: Joram, Ahaziah

Study Questions

• How did Jezebel take away Naboth's vineyard? (1 Kings 21:1-16)

• What was Elijah's stern prophecy about Jezebel's death? (1 Kings 21:23)

• How was Elijah's prophecy about Jezebel's death fulfilled? (2 Kings 9:30-37)

Joanna (joh-an-uh)

Joanna was a wealthy woman who helped support Jesus and his disciples. Her husband, Cuza, managed Herod Antipas' household. She and other women had been healed by Jesus. They believed in him and learned about God from him. In the Jewish culture at that time, women did not usually get as much education as men did. Jesus showed respect for women and showed that women and men are equally important to God. Joanna also was among the women who took spices to anoint Jesus' body after he was crucified. Two angels told them Jesus was alive. Joanna and the other women were the first to tell about Jesus' resurrection.

See Joanna's story in Luke 8:3 and 24:1-11.

Key event

Jesus' life, death, resurrection

Joash (joh-ash)

Joash was the boy king who had to be hidden away from his evil grandmother, Athaliah. Joash's father was King Ahaziah of Judah and his mother was Zibiah. Joash's grandmother Athaliah tried to kill all the royal family members so she could be queen. But Joash's aunt and uncle hid Joash away in the Temple. When he was seven, his uncle Jehoiada brought him out and crowned him king. As long as Jehoiada was alive, Joash obeyed God. He repaired the Temple, too. But after Jehoiada died, Joash followed bad advice. He killed Jehoiada's son and sent the Temple treasures to an enemy king as a bribe. Joash died dishonorably. His officials killed him.

See Joash's story in 2 Kings 11:1-12 and 2 Chronicles 22:11–24:27.

Key event

Reigns of Athaliah, Joash, and Amaziah

Job (johb)

Job was a great and wealthy man who lived in Uz. Uz was probably east of the Jordan River near Canaan, and Job probably lived about the time of Abraham.

Job loved the Lord and was kind and generous. He and his wife had seven sons and three daughters. Job always prayed for his family. But Satan told God that Job loved God only because he was rich and had an easy life. So God gave Satan permission to take away Job's blessings. All in one day, Job's wealth was stolen, and his servants and children were killed. Of course, Job cried and cried. But he also trusted in God. Satan then said Job would curse God if he lost his health. So God gave Satan permission to hurt Job but not kill him. Job's friends said he was being punished for sinning. But Job did not believe that, and in spite of all his tragedies and questions, he kept believing in God and his faithfulness.

See Job's story in the book of Job. See James 5:11 about his patience.

Key event
Time of the patriarchs

Relatives
Wife: Not named

Children: 20 unnamed sons and daughters; later: Jemimah, Keziah, Keren-Happuch

Study Questions
• What was unique and special about the way Job responded when he lost his children and health? (Job 1:13–2:13)

• How did God restore Job? (Job 42:10-17)

Joel (joh-uhl)

Joel was a prophet to Judah during prosperous times. He warned people to turn back to God to avoid judgment. Joel prophesied a coming drought and plague of locusts that would destroy all the crops. He told the people to repent by weeping, praying, and fasting. But Joel also predicted happy times when God's Holy Spirit would be poured out on people. Not just prophets and judges would have the Holy Spirit. Hundreds of years later, after Jesus died and rose again, the apostle Peter quoted the prophet Joel and said part of his prophecy came true as people were becoming Christians.

See Joel's prophecy in the book of Joel. See Peter's words about Joel in Acts 2:16-21.

Key event
Reign of Joash

John (jon)

John was a fisherman with his
father, Zebedee, and his
brother James. John became
one of Jesus' first disciples. He
probably was the youngest
one. He was part of the inner
circle of disciples with James
and Peter. Jesus called John
and James "sons of thunder"
because they wanted to call
fire down on some people
who disagreed with them.
Later John became known as
the "beloved Apostle." John's
mother asked Jesus for special
places in heaven for her sons.
When Jesus was on the cross,

he asked John to take care of Jesus' mother, Mary. John wrote
the Gospel of John. He also wrote 1 John, 2 John, 3 John, and
Revelation.
See Matthew, Mark, Luke, John, and Acts for John's life.

Key event
Ministry of Jesus; early church

Relatives
Father: Zebedee

Mother: Salome
Brother: James

Study Questions

• What were John and Peter doing that bothered the Jewish leaders? (Acts 4:1-2)
• Why did John write down the things that Jesus said and did? (John 20:30-31)
• How much of Jesus' life did John record? (John 21:24-25)

John Mark (jon mark)

John Mark, or Mark, was Barnabas' cousin. He was probably the young man who ran away when Jesus was arrested. Christians in Jerusalem met in the home of John Mark and his mother. They were praying when Peter was in prison and the angel led him to freedom. John Mark went with Barnabas and Paul on their first missionary journey. But he did not go on the whole trip with

them. Paul did not trust John Mark the next time he and Barnabas planned a trip. Paul would not let John Mark go with them. Paul and Barnabas disagreed about him. So Barnabas took him on a separate trip. This doubled the ministry they did. Later, Paul changed his mind about John Mark. John Mark wrote the

Gospel of Mark for Christians in Rome to show that Jesus is the one true Son of God.

See Mark's story in Acts 12:23–13:13 and 15:36-39. See Colossians 4:10; Philemon 24; 1 Peter 5:13 for things Paul said about him.

Key event

Paul's first missionary journey

Relatives

Mother: Mary (a popular name)

Cousin: Barnabas

Study Questions

• What happened to the young man who ran away when Jesus was arrested? (Mark 14:51-52)

• How did Paul change his mind about John Mark?
(2 Timothy 4:11)

John the Baptist (jon the bap-tist)

John the Baptist was a special baby. His parents were old and childless. His father was a Jewish priest. His mother was a distant relative of Mary, Jesus' mother. John was set apart before birth by God to prepare the way for Jesus. John the Baptist was like the prophet, Elijah. He lived in the desert, wore unusual clothes, and ate locust and honey. He was fearless and spoke to the king about repenting. People went to the desert to hear him. Some people thought he was the Messiah, but John told them he wasn't. When Jesus walked by one day, John said, "Look! There is the Lamb of God!" John the Baptist was beheaded by King Herod for preaching about sin.

See John the Baptist's story in Matthew, Mark, Luke, and John. See Isaiah 40:3 and Malachi 4:5 for predictions about him. He is also mentioned by the church leaders in Acts 1:5; 10:37; 11:16; 13:24-25; and 19:3-4.

Key event
Birth of Jesus; Jesus' ministry

Relatives
Father: Zechariah
Mother: Elizabeth
Distant relative: Jesus

Study Question
• What sort of advice did John the Baptist have for the religious leaders of his day? (Matthew 3:7-12)

Jonah (joh-nuh)

Jonah was the prophet who tried to run away from God instead of preaching to the people of Nineveh. Jonah did not like his assignment. God told Jonah to preach to the Assyrian capital of Nineveh. Jonah wanted them to get God's judgment, not mercy, because the Assyrians had been cruel to Israel. Instead of obeying, Jonah took a ship on the Mediterranean Sea heading away from Nineveh. But a raging storm gave Jonah time to change his mind and obey. Then God sent a huge fish to rescue him from drowning. It was just as he thought—the Ninevites repented and God forgave them. Jonah was angry because God forgave them. But God is compassionate to all who repent.

See Jonah's story in the book of Jonah. Read Jesus' words about him in Matthew 12:39-41.

Key event

Reign of Jeroboam II

Jonathan (jon-uh-thuhn)

Jonathan was the oldest son of King Saul and the best friend of David. He loved his father and his friend. He knew that David was going to be the next king instead of himself. Still he was loyal to his good friend. Saul became jealous of David. Several times he tried to kill him. But Jonathan protected David. Jonathan knew that God was the one who chose David to be king. Jonathan trusted God's wisdom. Jonathan was a valiant soldier. One time he and his armor bearer killed 20 Philistines by themselves. Jonathan, his father Saul, and two of his brothers died on the same day in battle. David grieved for his dear friend.

See Jonathan's story in 1 Samuel 13–31.
Key event
Reign of Saul

Joseph (joh-seph) (son of Jacob)

Joseph was the favorite son of the patriarch, Jacob. Jacob gave him a beautiful robe, the kind worn by royalty. Joseph's brothers were jealous. Joseph had dreams about his brothers bowing down to him. He told his brothers his dreams. That made them

more angry at him. They hated him so much they decided to kill him! He begged them not to. Instead, they sold him to merchants going to Egypt. Then the brothers lied to their father. They said Joseph must have been killed by a wild animal. Jacob was heartbroken.

In Egypt, Joseph became a slave. He was falsely accused of wrong-doing. Then he was put into prison. But God helped Joseph understand dreams. Pharaoh had a dream and Joseph was able to interpret it for

him. Suddenly, Joseph became very important in Egypt. One day Joseph looked and there were his brothers bowing down to him—just as Joseph had dreamed many years before.
See Joseph's story in Genesis 30–50. See Hebrews 11:22 about Joseph's faith.

Key event
Time of the patriarchs; time of Jacob; Joseph saves Egypt from famine

Relatives
Parents: Jacob and Rachel
Eleven brothers: Gad, Asher, Reuben, Simeon, Levi, Judah, Issachar, Zebulun, Benjamin, Dan, Naphtali
One Sister: Dinah
Wife: Asenath
Sons: Manasseh and Ephraim

Study Questions
• What was Pharaoh's dream and Joseph's plan? (Genesis 41:28-40)
• How did Joseph treat his brothers when he knew they were sorry? (Genesis 50:15-21)

Joseph (joh-seph) (Mary's husband)

Joseph was a carpenter who lived in the town of Nazareth. He was a descendant of King David. He was engaged to be married to Mary when Mary first told him she was pregnant. At first Joseph was very sad about this, because he knew the baby was not his. But Joseph was a good and kind man. He wanted to obey God and he did not want to hurt Mary. He decided to break the engagement quietly. But God sent an angel to tell Joseph that the

baby was God's Son. God told Joseph to marry Mary. So Joseph gladly took care of Mary and her baby. Later, he and Mary had other children. What a special man Joseph was for God to choose him to be Jesus' earthly father!
See Matthew 1:16–2:23 and Luke 1:26–2:52 for Joseph's story.

Key event
Birth of Jesus

Relatives
Wife: Mary
Children: Jesus, James, Joseph, Judas, Simon, and daughters

Study Questions

• Why did Joseph give Mary's baby the name Jesus? (Matthew 1:21; Luke 2:21)
• After Jesus was born, what messages did God give Joseph through an angel in a dream? (Matthew 2:13-15, 19-23)
• In what specific ways did Joseph obey God? (Luke 2:21-24; 39-42)

Joseph of Arimathea (joh-seph uhv air-i-muh-thee-uh)
Joseph was an important member of the Jewish high council and a godly man waiting for the Kingdom of God. He was a secret

believer in Jesus and had not agreed with the council decision to have Jesus crucified. After Jesus died he asked Pilate for Jesus' body. Nicodemus, the man who visited Jesus at night, went with Joseph. They wrapped Jesus' body in strips of linen with myrrh and aloe spices. Then they placed him in a new tomb carved in the rock, a tomb that belonged to Joseph, and rolled a large stone in the entryway. Joseph and Nicodemus showed their devotion to Jesus in death.

See Joseph's story in Matthew 27:57-58; Mark 15:42-43; Luke 23:50-52; John 19:38-42.

Key event

Jesus' life, death, and resurrection

Joshua (josh-oo-uh)

Joshua was Moses' young assistant during the Exodus. He stayed close to Moses and learned from him. Joshua was the only person allowed to go partway up the mountain when Moses' received the Ten Commandments from God. He was one of the 12 men who spied out Canaan for the Israelites (Caleb was the other). Only he and Caleb gave a good report when they returned. They told the people to trust God to give them victory. That is why they were the only two of those who left Egypt who lived long enough to enter the Promised Land.

The Lord told Moses to set Joshua apart to be a leader. Moses told Joshua not to be afraid. God gave Joshua the spirit of wisdom. Joshua took Moses' place when Moses died. Joshua actually was the one who led the people into the Promised Land. **See the book of Joshua for his life story. See also Exodus 17:9-14; 24:13; Numbers 11:28; 13:1–14:45; Deuteronomy 1:38; 3:21; Judges 2:6-9; and 1 Kings 16:34 for more details on Joshua's life.**

Key event
The Exodus; entering the Promised Land
Relatives
Father: Nun
Study Questions
• What made Joshua a hero? (Joshua 1:1-5)
• What happened when Joshua failed to ask the Lord for advice about the people of Gibeon? (Joshua 9:1-27)

Judah (joo-duh)

Judah was Jacob's fourth son, the first in the tribe of Israel through which King David and Jesus would come. Leah was Judah's mother. When Judah was younger he was the one who suggested selling his younger brother Joseph into slavery. He did not care much for his brother or his father. But later, when the sons of Jacob went to Egypt to buy grain, Judah was much more considerate of his father's feelings. He had seen his father grieve over losing Joseph. Jacob gave Judah the birthright blessing, even though he was not the oldest.

See Judah's story in Genesis 29:35–50:26.

Key event

Time of the patriarchs; time of Jacob; time of Joseph's rule in Egypt

Judas Iscariot (joo-duhss is-kair-ee-uht)

Judas was one of Jesus' 12 disciples. Jesus chose him just as he chose the others. Judas was the treasurer for the group. But he stole the money. He was a thief.

Judas lived and traveled with Jesus and the other disciples for three years. He heard Jesus preach, watched him heal sick people, and knew Jesus raised people from death. Still, Judas betrayed Jesus to the leaders who wanted him dead. They paid him 30 pieces of silver for Jesus, the price of a slave. Jesus knew what Judas was planning to do. But Jesus did not stop Judas. He knew that God was in control and that it was part of God's plan.

Judas ended his life as badly as he lived it. He felt terrible after betraying Jesus.

He went back to Jesus' enemies and tried to return the money they had paid him. But they refused it. Judas felt hopeless and killed himself.

See the story of Judas in Matthew, Mark, Luke, John, and in Acts 1:16-26.

Key event
Jesus's life, death, and resurrection

Relatives
Father: Simon

Study Questions
• Why did Judas speak harshly to Martha's sister Mary? (John 12:1-6)
• How did Jesus treat Judas even though he knew about the betrayal? (Matthew 26:20-25; John 13:21-30)

Jude (jood)

Jude was the brother of James, Joseph, Simon, and Jesus. Jesus was actually their half brother. Mary was their mother but Jesus' father was God. Joseph, Mary's husband, was the father of the other children. Jude, like his other brothers, at first did not believe Jesus was the Messiah. But after Jesus' death and resurrection, he joined Jesus' disciples. Jude wrote the book of Jude to warn believers about false teachers. He wanted people to be strong in their faith in Jesus Christ and to stand up for God's truth. Jude became a strong leader in the early church.

See Jude's story in Matthew 13:53-57; Mark 6:1-6; Acts 1:13-14; Jude 1.

Key event
Jesus' life; the early church

Judith (joo-dith)

Judith was one of Esau's wives. She was the daughter of Beeri the Hittite. The Hittites were pagans. They worshiped idols instead of the true God. God told the Israelites not to marry the people in Canaan. Esau did not obey God. This caused many problems for his family. "Esau's wives made life miserable for Isaac and Rebekah," his parents (Genesis 26:35). It was so bad that Rebekah said she'd rather die than to see Jacob, her other son, marry a Hittite woman.

See Judith's short story in Genesis 26:34-35; 27:46.

Key event
Time of the patriarchs; time of Isaac

Keturah (kuh-**too**-ruh)

Keturah was Abraham's wife after Sarah died. Keturah and Abraham had six sons. These sons were not part of the line of

the Messiah, or Redeemer. Her sons were Zimram, Jokshan, Medan, Midian, Ishbak, and Shuah. Abraham gave gifts to these sons while he was still alive, but they did not receive part of his inheritance. Isaac was the son of promise who received the inheritance. But Keturah and her sons became ancestors of the Midianites. Moses' wife and father-in-law were Midianites.

See Keturah's life in Genesis 25:1-8 and 1 Chronicles 1:32.

Key event
Time of the patriarchs; time of Abraham

Leah (lee-uh)

Leah was Jacob's first wife. Her father, Laban, had tricked Jacob into marrying her. In Leah and Jacob's time and place, men paid a dowry for a wife. Jacob had no money, so he worked seven years to marry Rachel, Leah's younger sister. Instead, behind the heavy wedding veil was Leah! Laban didn't tell Jacob that it was the custom for the oldest daughter to be married first. Jacob married Rachel second after working another seven years.

Leah never felt loved by Jacob. God gave her and Jacob six sons and a daughter. But she and Rachel were always jealous of each other. After she died, Jacob buried Leah in the cave of Machpelah in Hebron with Abraham, Sarah, Isaac, and Rebekah.

See Leah's story in Genesis 29:1–35:29; 49:31.

Key event

Time of the patriarchs; time of Isaac; time of Jacob

Lot (lot)

Lot was Abraham's nephew. Lot's father died, so Lot left Ur of the Chaldeans with Abraham and headed for Canaan. There Lot chose the best land for himself. Then he moved into the city of

Sodom, where the people lived godless lives. Lot became a city official. He did not help the people know about God. Instead, his family learned to follow Sodom's sinful ways. Abraham prayed for Lot. God sent angels to rescue Lot and his family from Sodom before it was destroyed. But the family did not really want to leave. The angels told them to hurry away and not to look back. But Lot's wife disobeyed. She looked back at the burning sulphur and turned into a pillar of salt. Lot made several bad choices in life. Still, he trusted God. The apostle Peter called Lot "a righteous man" (2 Peter 2:7-8).

See Genesis 11–14 and 19 for Lot's story. See Luke 17:28-33 for more details about him.

Key event
Time of the patriarchs; time of Abraham; destruction of Sodom and Gomorrah

Relatives
Father: Haran
Uncle: Abraham
Wife and two daughters: unnamed

Study Questions

• How did Abram save Lot from captivity? (Genesis 14:14-16)
• How did people react when Lot tried to warn them to leave Sodom? (Genesis 19:12-14)

Luke (luke)

Luke was a physician who wrote the Gospel of Luke and the book of Acts. He wanted to make a clear, orderly account of the life of Jesus Christ, the apostles, and the early church. Luke was the first church historian. He traveled much of the time with the apostle Paul. Many times he said "we" as he wrote about their travels. He may have been Paul's personal physician. Luke was with Paul in Rome when Paul was imprisoned. Paul spoke of him as "dear Doctor Luke." Luke's Gospel shows Jesus as the perfect man. It is also filled with many songs of praise and joy.

See Luke's story in Luke 1:3; Acts (for example, 16:10); Colossians 4:14.

Key event
The early church

Lydia (lid-ee-uh)

Lydia was a wealthy businesswoman in Philippi who became a Christian when Paul told her the Good News of Christ. She was from Thyatira. Lydia sold purple dye and cloth which was worn by royalty and the wealthy. She worshiped God and joined other women on the outskirts of the city to pray. Paul and Barnabas went to that place of prayer and told the women about Jesus Christ. God helped Lydia understand and believe. Then she was baptized. She offered her home and wealth to help Paul and the others traveling with him so they could preach in Philippi.

See Lydia's story in Acts 16:11–40.

Key event

Paul's second missionary journey

Malachi (mal-uh-kye)

Malachi was the last Old Testament prophet to the Israelites. In Jerusalem, the Temple had been rebuilt and the city walls had been rebuilt. But the people were losing their enthusiasm and devotion to God. Malachi wanted his people to know that God loved them. He made it clear that there will be judgment for those who are hostile to God and blessings for those who love him. But he called people to be sorry for their sin with the promise of God's forgiveness. It was almost 500 years before any more words came from the Lord after Malachi's message.
See Malachi's prophecy in the book of Malachi.

Key event
Return from exile; birth of Jesus

Manasseh (muh-**nass**-uh)

Manasseh, son of King Hezekiah, was one of the most evil kings Judah ever had. He built lots of idols and worship centers for others to worship idols. He worshiped false gods such as Ashtoreth and Molech. He even sacrificed some of his own children to these false gods. He did this throughout most of his 55-year reign as king. God said that Manasseh was worse than the pagan, unbelieving people around him. But then he was captured by the Assyrians and became a prisoner. This made him realize he had been wrong. He turned away from his sin and asked God to forgive him. God did, and Manasseh got to go back to Judah and right many of the wrongs he had done.
See Manasseh's story in 2 Kings 21:1-18 and 2 Chronicles 32:33–33:20. See Jeremiah 15:4 for some comments on how his life affected the nation of Judah.

Key event
Reigns of Hezekiah, Manasseh, and Amon

Mary (mair-ee) (Jesus' mother)

Mary was a young woman who lived in Nazareth when she first heard that she would be the mother of Jesus. She was engaged to Joseph, a carpenter. She loved God and carefully obeyed him. Like other people in Israel, Mary was waiting for the Messiah. The angel Gabriel told her she would be the mother of the Messiah, God's Son. Mary wondered how she could be pregnant since she was a virgin. But the angel told her that the Holy Spirit would do a miracle; the baby would be God's own Son. Mary praised God. Then God sent an angel to Joseph to explain everything to him. God used Mary and Joseph to take care of his Son, Jesus. Later, they had other children who were Jesus' half brothers and half sisters. Mary was the mother of Jesus but he was also her Savior. **See Mary's story in Matthew 1:16–2:23; Mark 3:31-32; 6:3; Luke 1:26-56; 2:1-52,**

and John 2:1-12. See Acts 1:14 for the last word about Mary.

Key event
Jesus' birth, death, and resurrection

Relatives
Husband: Joseph
Children: Jesus, James, Joseph, Judas, Simon, and daughters
Relatives: Zechariah and Elizabeth

Study Questions
• What did Matthew say regarding the prophecy about Jesus' birth? (Isaiah 7:14; Matthew 1:18-25)
• What were the words of the song Mary sang to the Lord? (Luke 1:46-55)

Mary and Martha (mair-ee and mar-thuh)

Mary, Martha, and their brother Lazarus were close friends of Jesus. Jesus often stayed in their home in Bethany. Martha was

the oldest of the sisters. She and Mary both believed that Jesus was the Messiah. But Martha liked to have everything just perfect. One time she was busy preparing food for Jesus. She got upset with all the work. She thought Mary should be helping her. Instead, Mary liked to sit at Jesus' feet and listen to him talk. Martha got so angry that she complained to Jesus about Mary. But Jesus said Mary had chosen the better thing to do. Another time, Mary poured expensive perfume on Jesus' head and feet. Then she wiped his feet with her hair. Some disciples thought it was a waste of money. But Jesus said Mary did a beautiful thing for him. She was preparing his body for burial before his death.

See Mary and Martha's story in Matthew 26:6-13; Mark 14:3-9; Luke 10:38-42; John 11:17-45; 12:1-11.

Key event
Jesus' ministry; death of Lazarus

Relatives
Mary and Martha were sisters
Brother: Lazarus

Study Questions
• What did Martha and Mary each say to Jesus about Lazarus' death? (John 11:1-44)
• How did Martha change her way of serving Jesus? (John 12:1-3)

Mary Magdalene (mair-ee mag-duh-leen)

Mary from Magdala, called Mary Magdalene, was devoted to Jesus for forgiving her sins and casting seven demons out of her. She helped support him and his disciples with her own money. Mary traveled from Galilee to help Jesus. At Jesus' crucifixion, all the men except John ran away. But Mary Magdalene and the other women stayed. She watched to see where he was buried. On

Sunday morning Mary and some other women took spices to put on Jesus' body. It was Mary Magdalene who first saw the risen Christ. She was also one of the women who ran and told the disciples the Good News that Jesus was alive. **See Mary's story in Matthew 27:1–28:20; Mark 15:1–16:20; Luke 8:1-3; 23:1–24:53; and John 19:1–20:25.**

Key event
Jesus' ministry, death, and resurrection

<u>Matthew</u> (math-yoo)

Matthew was a disciple of Jesus. He was also known as Levi. Matthew had been a tax collector. Tax collectors worked for the Roman government. They were considered traitors because they collected money from their fellow Jews for the Romans. They collected more than the amount of the tax and kept the extra for themselves. So they were wealthy at their countrymen's expense. They were doubly hated. When Jesus called Matthew to be a disciple, Matthew left behind his way of life and his job. But he did not leave his friends. Instead, he threw a party and invited his tax collector friends, Jesus, and his disciples. Matthew wanted his friends to meet Jesus, his best friend and Savior. Later, Matthew wrote the Gospel of Matthew. He showed that Jesus is the Son of David, the King of the Jews. **See Matthew's story in Matthew, Mark, Luke, and John. See Acts 1:12-14 to learn what Matthew did after Jesus' death.**

Key event

Jesus ministry, death, and resurrection

Relatives

Father: Alphaeus

Study Questions

• What was the reaction of the Pharisees when Jesus went to a party for tax collectors? (Matthew 9:10-13; Mark 2:13-17)
• How did Jesus respond when the Pharisees' got angry at him for being with Matthew? (Matthew 9:10-13; Mark 2:13-17)

Mephibosheth (me-fib-oh-sheth)

Mephibosheth was the son of Jonathan and the grandson of King Saul. His father and grandfather were killed in battle when he was five years old. His nurse picked him up to flee but he fell and hurt both feet. He was crippled from then on. David had promised Jonathan that he would be kind to Jonathan's descendants. He kept his promise. After David became king, he gave Mephibosheth Saul's property. David also invited Mephibosheth to eat at the king's table just like his own sons. Mephibosheth was very grateful for King David's kindness to him and his family. **See Mephibosheth's story in 2 Samuel 4:4; 9:1-13; 16:1-4; 19:24-30.**

Key event
Reigns of Saul and David

Miriam (mihr-ee-uhm)

Miriam was the older sister of Moses and Aaron. She watched Moses when his mother put him in a basket in the Nile River. She was quick to think about getting a Hebrew woman (her mother!) to take care of the baby for the Egyptian princess who found him. God used Miriam to help Moses and Aaron lead the people out of Egypt. After they crossed the Red Sea, Miriam led the women in singing and dancing in praise to God. But Miriam also became jealous of Moses' leadership. She and Aaron said God spoke through them too. As a result, God gave Miriam leprosy. But Moses asked God to heal her. And he did.

See Miriam's story in Exodus 2; 15; Numbers 12; 20; and Micah 6:4.

Key event
Birth of Moses; the Exodus

Moses (moh-zuhss)

Moses was the son of Jewish slaves in Egypt and one of the greatest prophets Israel ever had. When he was born, his parents disobeyed Pharaoh's law to drown baby boys. They hid Moses in a waterproof basket along the river's edge. God protected him.

The princess found the basket and adopted Moses. Moses later chose his Jewish people rather than be a prince. But it took a long time before he was ready for the job God had for him. Moses became the Israelites' most important leader. He spoke for God to the people and to Pharaoh. He led God's people out of Egypt to the Promised Land. God gave Moses the Ten Commandments. Moses also wrote the Pentateuch, the first five books of the Bible. He was not allowed to go into the

Promised Land because he once lost his temper with the people and disobeyed God's strict instructions.

See Moses' story in the books of Exodus, Leviticus, Numbers, and Deuteronomy. See shorter stories in Acts 7:17-44 and Hebrews 11:23-29.

Key Event
Birth of Moses; the Exodus

Relatives
Father: Amram
Mother: Jochebed
Sister: Miriam
Brother: Aaron
Wife: Zipporah
Sons: Gershom, Eliezer

Study Questions
• How long did Moses stay in the desert before God used him? (Acts 7:30-34)
• On what occasion did Moses appear in the New Testament? (Matthew 17:1-8)

Naboth (nay-both)

Naboth was an innocent man who was killed for refusing to sell his vineyard to King Ahab. The king had many vineyards. But he wanted the one Naboth had. Naboth would not sell because it was part of his inheritance from his father. Queen Jezebel had some men lie about Naboth and say that he cursed God and the king. The officials of the city took Naboth outside the city and stoned him to death. The prophet Elijah told Ahab that he would die at the same spot that Naboth died, and that is exactly what happened.

See Naboth's story in 1 Kings 21:1-19.

Key event

Reign of Ahab and Jezebel

Naomi (nay-oh-mee)

Naomi was Ruth's mother-in-law. Naomi and Elimelech, her husband, and their sons Mahlon and Kilion were Israelites. They all moved to Moab because of famine in Israel. Mahlon married a Moabite woman named Ruth, and Kilion married a Moabite woman named Orpah. Then all three men died. Naomi was sad and wanted to return to her country. Ruth saw God's love in Naomi and wanted to go with her. She went with Naomi to her hometown of Bethlehem. Naomi was sad that her husband and sons had died. But Ruth took care of Naomi by working in the fields to gather grain. Naomi's relative ,Boaz, was kind to Ruth and then married her. Ruth had a son. God gave Naomi a new family.

See Naomi's story in the book of Ruth.

Key event

Time of the judges

Nathan (nay-thuhn)

Nathan was a prophet who advised King David. He was bold yet wise in knowing how to give advice to the king. When David sinned with Bathsheba, Nathan told a story about a rich man with many lambs stealing a poor man's only lamb. David became angry and said the rich man should die. Nathan looked at King David and said, "You are that man!" David admitted he had sinned and said he was sorry. Nathan spoke for God and told David he would not die but there

were terrible consequences. Nathan was faithful to God to tell such a hard message to powerful King David. He gave the king good advice on many such occasions.

See Nathan's story in 2 Samuel 7–24; 1 Kings 1. He is also mentioned in 1 Chronicles 17:15 and 2 Chronicles 9:29; 29:25.

Key event

Reign of David

Nathanael (nuh-**than**-ee-uhl)

Nathanael, or Bartholomew, was one of Jesus' disciples. He was from Cana in Galilee. Philip was excited about finding "the very one Moses and the prophets wrote about." He went to find his friend, Nathanael. Philip told Nathanael that Jesus was from Nazareth. Nathanael was skeptical. He did not think anything good could come from that town. There was a Roman army garrison there. The Jews did not like the Romans. But Philip persisted and asked Nathanael to go and see for himself. Nathanael was surprised when Jesus said he had seen him sitting under a fig tree before Philip found him. Nathanael's doubt turned to strong faith in the Lord Jesus.

See Nathanael's story in John 1:45-51 and the disciples' names in Mark 3:13-19.

Key event

Jesus' ministry

Nebuchadnezzar (**neb**-uh-kuhd-**nez**-ur)

Nebuchadnezzar was the great Babylonian king who captured Jerusalem and exiled the Jews to Babylonia. At one time he had the most powerful army in the world. He ruled a vast empire. His Hanging Gardens of Babylon were one of the Seven Wonders of the Ancient World. Nebuchadnezzar was the king

who defeated the kingdom of Judah. Nebuchadnezzar was a very powerful man.

But he was also very proud, and God judged him for his conceit. Once Nebuchadnezzar had a disturbing dream. He could not remember what it was, so he ordered his wise men to tell him what he dreamed. He was going to kill them all if they didn't. Daniel was one of the exiles from Judah. God helped Daniel tell the king his dream and what it meant. It told how Nebuchadnezzar would go insane and eat grass like an animal. It happened just as Daniel predicted.

See Nebuchadnezzar's story in 2 Kings 24–25; 2 Chronicles 36; Jeremiah 21–52; and Daniel 1–4.

Key event

Reign of Jehoiakim; destruction of Jerusalem; the Exile

Relatives

Father: Nabopolassar
Son: Evil-Merodach
Grandson: Belshazzar

Study Questions

• What happened when Nebuchadnezzar ordered everyone to worship a large, golden idol? (Daniel 3:1-30)

• What happened to Nebuchadnezzar when he boasted his great power? (Daniel 4:28-37)

Nehemiah (nee-uh-**mye**-uh)

Nehemiah was the cupbearer for King Artaxerxes in Persia. He tasted the wine before giving it to the king to be sure it was safe and good. This was a trusted position. Nehemiah was a Jew in exile. He learned that the city wall around Jerusalem was ruined. Even after the Temple had been repaired, the wall was still broken down. Nehemiah gathered his courage by praying to God and then he talked to the king. He asked if he could go to Jerusalem and help the people get busy and build the wall. King Artaxerxes gave Nehemiah permission to go. He also gave him letters so that he could have help with the work. Nehemiah was a soldier, a statesman, and the governor of Jerusalem. In everything he did, Nehemiah prayed and asked God to help him or prayed and gave God thanks.

See Nehemiah's story in the book of Nehemiah.

Key event
The Exile; return to Jerusalem

Relatives
Father: Hacaliah

Study Questions
• What did Nehemiah do when enemies tried to ruin the work? (Nehemiah 4:1-23)
• Why was it significant that Nehemiah and the people rebuilt the walls in record time? (Nehemiah 6:15-16)
• How did Nehemiah help everyone worship God the right way? (Nehemiah 13:30-31)

Nicodemus (nik-uh-**dee**-muhss)

Nicodemus was a Jewish teacher and a Pharisee. Pharisees were a group of religious leaders in Israel during the time of Jesus. Most of them did not believe Jesus was God's Son. Nicodemus went to talk to Jesus at night to find out for himself what Jesus had to say. Jesus told Nicodemus that a person must be born again to enter the Kingdom of God.

Nicodemus had a hard time under-standing Jesus. But later Nicodemus tried to get the other Pharisees at least to listen to Jesus. They made fun of Nicodemus. But by the time Jesus had been crucified on the cross, Nicodemus was a believer in him. After Jesus died, Nicodemus went with Joseph of Arimathea to ask Pilate for the body of Jesus. The two men buried Jesus in a tomb close to the place where Jesus was crucified.

See the story of Nicodemus in John 3:1-21; 7:50-52; 19:39-40.

Key event
Ministry and death of Jesus

Relatives
None mentioned

Study Questions
• What well-known verse comes from the conversation Jesus had with Nicodemus? (John 3:1-21)
• What did Nicodemus' fellow Pharisees think of him? (John 7:32-52)

Noah (noh-uh)

Noah was the man whom God saved from the Flood. He loved and obeyed God. Noah lived before written history, probably near the garden of Eden. At that time God was sorry he had made people. They had become always evil and violent. So God decided to destroy the earth. But God had a plan to save Noah's family and pairs of all the animals. God told Noah to build a large boat, or ark. It took Noah and his sons 120 years to build it. It was 137 meters long and 23 meters wide. Other people must have asked Noah what he was doing. But no one else believed God or went into the Ark with Noah and his family. God kept his word and sent a flood to destroy the world. He also kept his word to save Noah and his family.

See Noah's story in Genesis 5:29–10:32. See Hebrews 11:7; 1 Peter 3:20; and 2 Peter 2:5 for more descriptions of Noah and his time.

Key event
Creation; the Flood

Relatives
Grandfather: Methuselah
Father: Lamech
Wife: Not named
Sons: Shem, Ham, and Japheth

Study Questions
• How did Noah gather the animals? (Genesis 6:20)
• How did Noah respond to God's instructions? (Genesis 6:22; 7:5)
• What promise did God make after the Flood? (Genesis 9:8-17)

Onesimus (oh-**nes**-i-muhss)

Onesimus was a slave who ran away, learned about Jesus, and became a Christian. He was Philemon's slave, but he ran away to

Rome. There Onesimus met the apostle Paul who told him about Jesus. After a while Onesimus understood that he should return to his owner. Paul sent a letter to Philemon asking him to receive his slave like a Christian brother instead of a thing that Philemon owned. Onesimus means "useful." Paul said that before his salvation Onesimus wasn't very useful to Philemon. But since he became a Christian he was very useful both to Paul and to Philemon. Paul said Onesimus was like a son to him. **See the letter about Onesimus in the book of Philemon.**

Key event
The early church; Paul's journey to Rome

Onesiphorus (**oh**-ne-**si**-for-uhss)

Onesiphorus was a Christian and a good friend to the apostle Paul. Some of Paul's friends and helpers left him alone when he was in prison in Rome. Perhaps they were ashamed or frightened to be his friend. But Onesiphorus went looking for Paul when he was in prison. He made Paul feel better and cheered him up.

Perhaps he took him good food or a warm blanket. Maybe Onesiphorus sang and prayed with Paul. He also helped him in many ways when he was working in Ephesus. Paul sent warm greetings to Onesiphorus in his second letter to Timothy.
See Paul's words about Onesiphorus in 2 Timothy 1:16-18; 4:19.

Key event
The early church; Paul's journey to Rome

Paul (pawl)

Paul was the first great missionary of the Christian church. His Jewish name was Saul, and he was from the city of Tarsus. Before he believed in Jesus, he was a Pharisee, a Jew who strictly kept the Old Testament law. He hated Christians and thought he was pleasing God to hurt them. Then the resurrected Jesus appeared to Saul in a blinding light. Saul realized that Jesus really is God and that the Christians were right. Saul believed and started using all his energy to tell people about Jesus. He went on three missionary journeys to take the Good News throughout the Roman Empire. He wrote 13 of the New Testament books. Some of them are Romans, Galatians, Ephesians, 1 Timothy, and 2 Thessalonians. Paul was beaten, stoned, flogged, arrested, thrown into prison, and executed for his faith in Jesus Christ. **See Paul's story in Acts 7:58–28:31 and in his many New Testament letters.**

Key event

The early church; Paul's first missionary journey; Paul's second missionary journey; Paul's third missionary journey; Paul's journey to Rome

Relatives
None mentioned
Study Questions
• What was Saul doing when Stephen was stoned?
(Acts 7:54-60)
• What did God tell Ananias to do for Saul? (Acts 9:1-19)
• How did Lydia hear Paul's message about Jesus?
(Acts 16:11-15)

Peninnah (puh-nin-uh)

Peninnah was a woman who lived during the time of the judges
of Israel. She was married to Elkanah and she had many children.
Elkanah had another wife named Hannah who had no children.
Peninnah was very unkind to Hannah. Peninnah made fun of her
because she had no children. Hannah would get so upset she
couldn't eat. Peninnah may have been jealous of Hannah because
Elkanah loved Hannah best. God had said families should be
made of just one husband and one wife. Otherwise there are a
lot of problems.
See Peninnah's story in 1 Samuel 1.

Key event
Time of the Judges

Peter (pee-tur)

Peter was a fisherman who became a close disciple of Jesus.
Peter's brother Andrew introduced him to Jesus. At first he was
called Simon. But Jesus called him Peter, meaning "rock." Peter,
James, and John became the inner circle of Jesus' followers. They

saw Jesus raise Jairus' daughter from death. He saw Jesus in his glory on a mountain.

Peter was very enthusiastic about Jesus. He was the first of the disciples to say that Jesus was the Messiah. Once when Jesus told the disciples he was going to die and they would desert him,

Peter said, "No! Even if I have to die with you! I will never deny you!" But he did deny Jesus—three times while Jesus was on trial. Then Peter cried. He was very sad to have let down his close friend and Savior.

After Jesus rose from the dead, he appeared to the disciples. They were sorry for deserting him and he forgave them. Peter became a strong leader in the early church. He wrote the books of 1 Peter and 2 Peter.

See Peter's story in Matthew, Mark, Luke, John, and Acts.

Key event
Jesus' ministry, death, and resurrection; early church

Relatives
Father: John
Brother: Andrew

Study Questions
• How did Peter become a disciple of Jesus? (Matthew 4:18-20)
• How did Peter get himself in trouble with Jesus? (Matthew 16:21-23)
• How did Peter act after Jesus' resurrection? (Acts 4:13-20; 5:27-32)

Philemon (fye-**lee**-muhn)

Philemon was a wealthy Greek landowner who became a Christian because of Paul's teaching. The church in Colosse met in his home. Paul wrote him a letter. He praised Philemon for his faith and love and for helping other Christians. Then Paul asked Philemon to accept his slave Onesimus back like a Christian brother. Paul wanted to keep Onesimus with him, but he wanted Philemon to freely forgive Onesimus. Paul asked Philemon to welcome Onesimus the way he would welcome Paul himself. Paul also told Philemon that he would pay any debts that Onesimus owed. But Paul reminded Philemon that he owed his very life to Paul for leading him to Christ.

See Paul's letter to Philemon.

Key event
Paul's journey to Rome; the early church

Philip (fil-ip)

Philip was a Greek-speaking Jew who served as a deacon and then as an evangelist in the early church. As a deacon he helped give food to the poor. Later the Christians were scattered because of persecution. Philip went to Samaria and spoke about Christ wherever he went. He healed people of diseases and evil spirits, and he understood and could explain Scripture to others. An angel of the Lord sent Philip to the desert where he helped a man understand the Bible and then baptized him. Afterward, the Spirit of the Lord took Philip away. Philip was one of the first traveling missionaries.

See Philip's story in Acts 6:1-7; 8:5-40; 21:8-10.

Key event
Paul's first missionary journey; the early church

Phoebe (fee-bee)

Phoebe was a believer and a deaconess in the church in Cenchrea. A deaconess serves in the church by helping the needy. Cenchrea was the eastern port of Corinth. Phoebe may have personally delivered the apostle Paul's letter to the Romans, which he wrote while in Corinth. In that letter he asks the church at Rome to receive Phoebe warmly and help her in any way she needs. Phoebe was helpful to many people including Paul. Perhaps she was wealthy and helped support the ministry of Paul as he taught the Corinthian church.

See the short story of Phoebe in Romans 16:1-2.

Key event
The early church

Pontius Pilate (pon-shus pye-luht)

Pontius Pilate was the Roman governor of Judea during Jesus' death. When the Jewish leaders wanted to crucify Jesus they needed Pilate's authority. They took Jesus before Pilate for questioning and sentencing. Three times Pilate said that Jesus was not guilty. Pilate's wife had a strange dream and told Pilate to have nothing to do with Jesus. But Pilate didn't listen. Every Passover he set a prisoner free. He offered Jesus. But the people called for Barabbas, a thief and murderer. Finally, Pilate washed his hands in front of everyone. He said he was not responsible for Jesus' death. Pilate knew what was right to do but he was afraid of the people.

See **Pilate's story in Matthew 27:11-26 and Mark 15:1-15.**

Key event
Jesus' death

Potiphar (pot-uh-fur)

Potiphar was the Egyptian official who bought Joseph from the Midianite slave traders. Potiphar was the captain of the guard for Pharaoh. He was very rich because of his high position. His house was probably two or three stories tall with elaborate gardens and balconies—much more than most people had. Expensive works of art and gold plates filled the rooms. Potiphar noticed that the Lord blessed everything Joseph did. So he put Joseph in charge of his household. As a result, Potiphar and his household were blessed, too. Joseph continued to trust God even when Potiphar's wife lied about Joseph and Potiphar threw him in prison. After all, Potiphar had to believe his wife.

See Potiphar's story in Genesis 39:1-20.

Key event
Time of the patriarchs; Joseph in slavery in Egypt

Rachel (ray-chuhl)

Rachel was the favorite wife of Jacob. In Old Testament times some men had many wives. It was not God's plan, but some people did it. And it often caused many problems. Jacob worked for Rachel's father for seven years in order to marry her. But Rachel's father tricked Jacob and gave Leah to him. Jacob loved Rachel so much that he agreed to work another seven years for permission

to marry her! For a long time Rachel could not have any children. She was jealous of Leah, who did have children. She was afraid that Jacob loved Leah more, and she argued with her sister and her husband. Later, God let Rachel have two sons, Joseph and Benjamin. But Rachel died soon after Benjamin was born. Rachel's sons became Jacob's favorite children. In Ruth 4:11, Rachel's name is used as a blessing. In the book of Jeremiah (31:15) and the book of Matthew (2:18) she is named as the mother of all Israel.

See Rachel's story in Genesis 29:1–35:20.

Key event

Time of the patriarchs; time of Joseph

Relatives
Father: Laban
Aunt: Rebekah
Sister: Leah
Husband: Jacob
Sons: Joseph and Benjamin

Study Question
• How did Rachel feel about leaving home with Jacob? (Genesis 31:14-16)
• Where was Rachel buried? (Genesis 35:19)

Rahab (ray-hab)

Rahab was a woman in Jericho who hid two Israelite spies when the Israelites began conquering the Promised Land. The people in Jericho worshiped idols. Rahab knew that Joshua and the Israelite army were going to destroy her city. Everyone was terrified. But Rahab put her trust in the Lord. She asked the spies to save her and her family. They told her to put a red cord in her window. Everyone in her house with the red cord would be safe. Rahab obeyed. When the walls of Jericho fell, the Israelites saved Rahab and her family. Rahab later married Salman and became the mother of Boaz. Her faith brought her into God's family. She became an ancestor of King David.

See Rahab's story in Joshua 2:1-23; 6:22-23; Hebrews 11:31.

Key event
The Exodus; entering the Promised Land

Rebekah (re-bek-uh)

Rebekah was Isaac's wife. She was an answer to prayer. Abraham wanted a bride for his son Isaac. But he did not want Isaac to marry a Canaanite woman who worshiped idols. So Abraham sent his servant back to Haran to find a wife for Isaac. The servant asked God to lead him to the right person and God did. The woman was Rebekah. She agreed to return and marry Isaac.

At first she could not have any children. Then Isaac prayed for his wife and God gave them twins, Esau and Jacob. The Lord told Rebekah that the younger one would rule the older. Rebekah did not pray or wait to see what God would do. Instead, she had Jacob trick his father, Isaac. Jacob received the blessing that the older son should have received. Of course, Esau was so angry he threatened to kill Jacob. Jacob had to run away. Rebekah lost a lot to get what she wanted. **See Rebekah's story in Genesis 24:1–27:46; 49:31.**

Key event
Time of the patriarchs; time of Abraham

Relatives
Grandparents: Nahor and Milcah
Father: Bethuel
Husband: Isaac
Brother: Laban
Twin sons: Esau and Jacob

Study Question
• How did God lead Abraham's servant to Rebekah? (Genesis 24:12-27)

Rhoda (roh-duh)

Rhoda was a young servant girl who was so excited to hear Peter's voice at the door that she forgot to let him in! Rhoda served in the house of John Mark's mother, Mary. The believers were gathered there to pray for Peter's release from prison. King Herod had executed the apostle James and he had arrested Peter. The believers did not want Peter executed, too. While they were praying, God was answering their prayers. An angel took Peter out of prison. Peter went to Mary's house. But even though they were praying, Rhoda was surprised to hear Peter at the door. The others did not believe her. Finally they let Peter in.

See Rhoda's funny story in Acts 12:1-17.

Key event
The early church

Ruth (rooth)

Ruth was a young woman from Moab who became the great-grandmother of King David. Her story begins with a famine in Judah. A man from Bethlehem took Naomi, his wife, and two sons to Moab to find food. The man died and his sons married Moabite women. One was Orpah and the other was Ruth. Then Naomi's sons died, also. Naomi decided to return to Bethlehem. She kissed her daughters-in-law good bye and told them to return to their own mothers. But Ruth refused. She wanted to go with Naomi. She wanted to serve Naomi's God, the true Lord, instead of the false gods of Moab. Ruth promised to take care of Naomi. She gathered the leftover grain from the farmers' fields. A wealthy farmer named Boaz noticed Ruth. He learned that she was kind and faithful to her mother-in-law. Boaz asked Ruth to marry him. He and Ruth took care of Naomi.

See Ruth's story in the book of Ruth. She is also mentioned in Jesus' genealogy in Matthew 1:5.

Key event
Time of the Judges

Relatives
Parents-in-law: Elimelech and Naomi
First husband: Mahlon
Second husband: Boaz

Study Question
• Where did Ruth glean the fields? (Ruth 2:19-23)

Salome (suh-loh-mee) (wife of Zebedee)

Salome was the mother of James and John. She was from Galilee. Salome was one of the women who followed Jesus and helped provide for his needs. She asked Jesus to give her sons honored places in his kingdom. At Jesus' crucifixion, all the men but John ran away. Salome and the other women stayed with Jesus. Salome was also one of the women who went to the tomb on Sunday morning to put sweet spices on Jesus' body. She saw the angels and heard the Good News that Jesus was alive. She went with Mary Magdalene and another Mary to tell the disciples. **See Salome's story in Matthew 20:20-21; 27:56; Mark 15:40; 16:1.**

Key event

Jesus' ministry, death, and resurrection

Salome (suh-loh-mee) (Herodias' daughter)

Salome was the young woman who asked for John the Baptist's head on a platter. Salome was the daughter of Herodias and the step-daughter of Herod the Tetrarch. She danced at Herod's birthday party. He was so pleased with her that he said she could have almost anything she wanted. She asked her mother's advice. Her mother hated John the Baptist because he spoke against her sin, so she told Salome to ask for John's head! Herod did not want to kill John, but he also did not want to look foolish to his guests. So Salome got what she wanted. Salome's name is not mentioned, but Josephus, a Jewish historian, identifies her. **See Salome's story in Matthew 14:3-12 and Mark 6:17-29.**

Key event
Jesus' ministry; John the Baptist's death

Samson (sam-suhn)

Samson was a judge in Israel known for his great strength. Before he was born, an angel told his mother to set him apart as a Nazirite. He was never to cut his hair, touch a dead body, or drink alcohol, not even once. God gave Samson great physical strength.

He was supposed to use his strength to rescue his people from the Philistines. Samson once killed a lion with his bare hands. He even killed 1,000 Philistines with the jawbone of a donkey. But he often used his strength for personal revenge. Also, Samson made bad choices when it came to women. In fact, a Philistine woman named Delilah tricked him into telling her the source of his strength. While he slept, she had someone shave

his head, breaking his Nazirite vow. The Lord took his strength away and the Philistines captured Samson.

See Samson's story in Judges 13–16. In spite of his failures, Samson is still in the list of those who had faith in God. See Hebrews 11:32.

Key Event
Time of the Judges

Relatives
Father: Manoah
Mother and brothers unnamed

Study Questions
• What did the Philistines do to Samson? (Judges 16:21)
• How did God use Samson in spite of his failures? (Judges 16:22-31)

Samuel (sam-yoo-uhl)

Samuel was Israel's last judge and also a priest and prophet. His name means "asked of God" because Hannah, his mother, had prayed desperately for a son before he was born. When Samuel was a child, Hannah took him to the tabernacle and gave him back to the Lord. He lived there with Eli, the high priest.

God called Samuel to be a prophet when he was still a boy. It happened late at night while everyone was sleeping. The Lord spoke to Samuel. Samuel thought Eli was calling him, so he ran to see what he wanted. This happened three times. Then Eli told Samuel it was God calling him. Eli told Samuel to answer, "Yes, Lord, your servant is listening."

Samuel was devoted to obeying God. He grew up and became the next priest. He anointed the first two kings of Israel (Saul and David), and he spoke to the people for God. But his own two sons did not follow his faith in the Lord.
See Samuel's life in 1 Samuel 1–28 and Psalm 99:6. See Acts 3:24 and 13:20 for his place in Jewish history, and Hebrews 11:32 for his place among the faithful.

Key event
Time of the judges; reign of Saul

Relatives
Mother: Hannah
Father: Elkanah
Siblings: three younger brothers and two sisters
Sons: Joel and Abijah

Study Question
• What warning did Samuel give the people after they had a king? (1 Samuel 12:16-25)

Sanballat (san-bal-uht)

Sanballat was the governor of Samaria when Nehemiah returned to Jerusalem to rebuild the city walls. Sanballat, Tobiah, and

Geshem were rulers in the surrounding areas of Jerusalem. They did not want Nehemiah and the other Jews to rebuild the wall. Sanballat accused Nehemiah of rebelling against King Artaxerxes. Sanballat mocked the Jews and made fun of their work. He said the wall would fall down easily. Then Sanballat threatened Nehemiah and the workers. Later when the wall was completed, Sanballat was angry. He tried to scare Nehemiah away by hiring a false prophet. Nehemiah prayed and kept trusting the Lord to deal with Sanballat as God saw fit.

See Sanballat's story in Nehemiah 2; 4; 6.

Key event

Rebuilding the walls of Jerusalem

Sarah (sair-uh)

Sarah, or Sarai, was the woman God chose to be the mother of the Israelite nation. She was the wife of Abram, or Abraham. They married in Ur of the Chaldeans, then moved to Canaan. God promised Abraham and Sarah that they would become a great nation. But Sarah and Abraham were getting older and they still had no children. Sarah then took matters into her own hands. She gave her servant girl to Abraham as a wife. She thought this was OK because other women did it, but it was not wise. This caused many problems in Sarah's family. Finally when she was 90 years old, Sarah had a baby, Isaac! This shows that Sarah was special to God, too, not just Abraham. He wanted this son to be their son. Sarah lived to be 127 years old.

See Sarah's story in Genesis 11:25 and Isaiah 51:2. The promise was to come through both Abraham and Sarah: Romans 9:8-9. In Hebrews 11:11 Sarah is the first woman

in the Hall of Faith. 1 Peter 3:6 gives her as an example of a godly wife.

Key event
Time of the patriarchs

Relatives
Father: Terah
Husband: Abraham
Half brothers: Nahor and Haran
Nephew: Lot
Son: Isaac

Study Question
• Why did Sarah laugh and lie about it? (Genesis 18:10-15)

Saul (sawl)

Saul was the first king of Israel. The people wanted to have a king like other nations. So God told the prophet Samuel to anoint Saul. Saul was handsome, impressive, and stood a head taller than most men. He was 30 years old when he became king.

Saul had many kingly qualities. But he often did not obey God. And he did not always mean it when he said he was sorry. One time Saul was supposed to wait for Samuel to come and make an offering to the Lord. Samuel was late and so Saul went ahead and made the sacrifice himself. Samuel said because of that, God would take the throne away from Saul. Saul was also jealous of David and tried to kill him several times. But David never tried to get him back. Saul reigned for 40 years. He and his son Jonathan were killed in battle by the Philistines.

See Saul's life in 1 Samuel 9–31 and Acts 13:21.

Key Event
Reigns of Saul and David

Relatives
Father: Kish
Wife: Ahinoam
Sons: Jonathan and Ishbosheth
Daughters: Merab and Michal (David married Michal)

Study Questions
• What did Saul learn the hard way? (1 Samuel 15:22-23)
• How did David prove his loyalty to Saul? (1 Samuel 24:1-22)

Shadrach, Meshach & Abednego
(**shad**-rak, **mee**-shuhk, uh-**bed**-nuh-goh)

Shadrach, Meshach, and Abednego were Israelite captives in Babylon like their friend Daniel. Their Hebrew names were Hananiah, Mishael, and Azariah. The Lord had given them wisdom so they were counted among the king's wise men. But Daniel's friends remained faithful to the Lord. When the king made a golden image and commanded everyone to fall down and worship it, the three young men simply refused. They knew the king would punish them by throwing them into a huge furnace. But they trusted God. The king's fury turned to amazement when the three Hebrew men were thrown into the furnace and

came out without even the smell of smoke on them.

See the story of Shadrach, Meshach, and Abednego in Daniel 1–3.

Key event
The Exile

Shaphan (shay-fuhn)

Shaphan was secretary to King Josiah of Judah. Hilkiah the high priest was cleaning out the Temple at the king's command. For years it had been neglected. Hilkiah found the Book of the Law. He told Shaphan and gave it to him. Shaphan reported to King Josiah all that was taking place in the clean up and repair of the Temple. Then he reported that Hilkiah found "a book." Shaphan wasn't sure what the king's reaction would be but he read from the Book of the Law. King Josiah was filled with sorrow to see how far his people had gone from worshiping the Lord.

See Shaphan's story in 2 Kings 22:1-12 and 2 Chronicles 38:8-20.

Key event
Reign of Josiah

Silas (sye-luhss)

Silas was a Christian who became a leader and a prophet in the early church. He was a Roman citizen living in Jerusalem. He was also called Silvanus. He was sent by the Jerusalem church to Antioch to assure the Gentile believers that they had nothing to worry about. (Some people had been saying that Gentiles had to become Jews before they could become followers of Jesus.) Silas also traveled with Paul on his second missionary journey. It was Silas who was thrown into jail with Paul for casting an evil spirit out of a girl. During the night Silas and Paul prayed and sang praises to God. God sent an earthquake that opened the prison doors. Later the jailer asked how he could be saved. Silas was also the writing secretary for Paul and Peter.

See the story of Silas in Acts 15:22–19:10. Paul and Peter also mention him in 2 Corinthians 1:19; 1 Thessalonians 1:1; 2 Thessalonians 1:1; and 1 Peter 5:12.

Key event
Early church; Paul's second missionary journey

Relatives
None mentioned

Study Questions
• What instructions did Silas and the others take to the Gentile believers? (Acts 15:23-29)
• What did the apostle Peter think of Silas? (1 Peter 5:12)

Simeon (sim-ee-uhn)

Simeon was an old man who recognized the infant Jesus as the Messiah whom God had promised. Simeon was waiting to see the Messiah because the Lord told Simeon he would not die until he saw him. When Mary and Joseph took Jesus to the Temple in Jerusalem to consecrate him, Simeon held the baby in his arms and praised the Lord for his salvation. Simeon predicted that some people would reject Jesus and some would accept him. He also said Mary would suffer. Simeon said he could die in peace since God let him see the Messiah. **See Simeon's story in Luke 2:25-35.**

Key event
Birth of Jesus

Simon the sorcerer (sye-muhn the sor-sur-ur)

Simon the sorcerer used magic and thought he could buy spiritual power. Simon lived in Samaria. He did many tricks and was boastful. Philip, one of the seven deacons, went to Samaria and was preaching the Good News of Christ. Simon believed in Jesus and was baptized. So many Samaritans were believing that Peter and John went to see what the Lord was doing. Peter and John layed their hands on the people and prayed for them to receive the Holy Spirit. When Simon saw that, he wanted to buy the power! Peter rebuked Simon and told him to repent and pray for God's forgiveness. Wisely, Simon asked Peter to pray for him. **See Simon's story in Acts 8:9-25.**

Key event
The early church

Solomon (sol-uh-muhn)

Solomon was the wisest man in the world in his day. He was King David's son, third king of Israel. He was also called Jedidiah, "loved by the Lord." God let Solomon build the magnificent Temple for the Lord.

Solomon started off well. God spoke to him in a dream and told him to ask for whatever he wanted. Solomon asked for wisdom to rule his people and to know the difference between right and wrong. God was so pleased with Solomon's request that he also gave him riches and honor. But Solomon did not always use the wisdom God gave him. He married many wives from foreign countries. They brought their idols with them and persuaded Solomon to worship them. He tells of the hard lessons he learned in the book of Ecclesiastes.

After Solomon died, God divided his kingdom. Solomon wrote many proverbs, some Psalms, Ecclesiastes, and Song of Songs.

See Solomon's life in 2 Samuel 12:24–24:25; 1 Kings 1:1–11:43.

Key event
Reigns of David and Solomon; building of the Temple

Relatives
Father: David
Mother: Bathsheba
Brothers: Absalom, Adonijah, others
Sister: Tamar
Son: Rehoboam

Study Questions
• What is the most famous example of Solomon's wisdom? (1 Kings 3:16-28)
• What did Nehemiah say about Solomon? (Nehemiah 13:26)

Stephanas (stef-uh-nuhss)

Stephanas and his household were the first people to become Christians in Achaia. Paul told them about Jesus and they believed in him as their Savior. Paul also baptized them. These Christians

used their time and energy to serve other Christians. Paul said the people in the church at Corinth should submit to such workers. Stephanas and some other men visited Paul and took him some things that helped him in a time of need.
See Paul's mention of Stephanas in 1 Corinthians 1:16; 16:15-18.

Key event
The early church

Stephen (steev-uhn)

Stephen was the first Christian martyr. He was one of the seven deacons in charge of giving food to the widows and poor. He was filled with the Holy Spirit, faith, grace and mercy. God enabled him to perform miracles to bless people. Stephen loved God and his Word and told many people about the Lord. But some of the Jews who feared the new Christians twisted Stephen's words and lied about him. They accused him of talking against God. Stephen reminded them of their history and said they had rejected their Messiah. But they were so angry that they dragged Stephen outside the city and stoned

him to death. While he was dying Stephen asked Jesus to forgive them.

See Stephen's story in Acts 6:3–8:2.

Key event
The early church

Susanna (soo-zan-uh)

Susanna was one of several women whom Jesus healed from diseases and helped in other ways. She was glad for all that Jesus had done for her. Susanna, Mary Magdalene, Joanna, and many other women traveled with Jesus and his disciples. Susanna and the other women were not allowed to do all the things that men were allowed to do. But they could provide money to buy food for Jesus and his followers. Jesus showed that everyone is important to God. Susanna and the other women wanted more people to hear the Good News that Jesus taught.

See Susanna's story in Luke 8:1-3.

Key event
Life, death, resurrection of Jesus

<u>Theophilus</u> (thee-ah-fil-uhss)

Theophilus was the person to whom Luke addressed his book of Luke and the book of Acts. The name Theophilus means "one who loves God." Theophilus was probably an important Roman friend of Luke who wanted to know all about Jesus and his followers. As a doctor, Luke paid attention to details. He told his friend that he carefully investigated all the facts. Then he wrote these books "to reassure you of the truth of all you were taught" (Luke 1:4).

See Luke's words to Theophilus in Luke 1:1-4 and Acts 1:1.

<u>*Key event*</u>
Jesus' ministry; early church

<u>Thomas</u> (tom-uhss)

Thomas was one of Jesus' 12 disciples, or apostles. His name

means "twin." Didymus was his Greek name. Thomas loved Jesus and was loyal to him. Thomas showed this one day when Jesus wanted to go to Bethany because Lazarus had died. The disciples knew the Jewish leaders wanted to kill Jesus. Thomas showed his courage by saying, "Let's go, too—and die with Jesus." But of course, like all the others, Thomas ran away when Jesus was arrested. And later he earned the name "Doubting

Thomas" because he said he would not believe Jesus was alive from the dead unless he put his finger in the nail holes. Of course, just seeing Jesus was enough. Thomas called Jesus, "My Lord and my God!"

See Thomas' story in Matthew, Mark, Luke, John, and Acts 1:13.

Key event

Jesus' ministry, death, and resurrection

Timothy (tim-uh-thee)

Timothy was a young missionary and pastor who learned from and traveled with the apostle Paul. He lived in Lystra and became a Christian when Paul taught there. Timothy then traveled with Paul on his other missionary journeys. He became like a son to Paul. Timothy's mother and grandmother were Christians, but his father was a Gentile. Timothy learned from Paul and served the churches with him. Paul encouraged Timothy to be faithful and strong. Two of Paul's letters to Timothy are part of the New Testament. Timothy was probably with Paul when he died.

See Timothy's story in Acts 16:1-5. Paul mentions him in many letters: Romans 16:21; 1 Corinthians 4:17; 16:10-11; Philippians 1:1; 2:19-23.

Key event
Paul's first missionary journey; Paul's journey to Rome; the early church

Titus (tye-tuss)

Titus was a young Gentile believer who was a helper to the apostle Paul. Titus was an example to the church that non-Jews could be faithful believers in Christ. Paul sent him to help solve

problems in the Corinthian church. Titus was a representative of Paul to the churches. Titus became a faithful pastor to churches in Crete and Dalmatia. Paul's letter to Titus is part of the New Testament. It gives instructions about leaders in the church.

See Paul's words about Titus in 2 Corinthians 2:13; 7:6-16; 8:6, 16-24; 12:18; Galatians 2:1-5; 2 Timothy 4:10. Paul's words to Titus are in the book of Titus.

Key event
Paul's first missionary journey; the early church

Trophimus (troh-fim-uhss)

Trophimus was a Gentile believer from Ephesus. He traveled with Paul and helped bring gifts of money to the Jewish believers in Jerusalem. Paul wanted Gentile Christians and Jewish Christians to love and trust each other. Some of the Jews who did not believe in Jesus thought Paul took Trophimus into the Temple. (He did not.) Since Trophimus was not Jewish, that would have been against the Jewish law. The leaders used this to stir up the crowd. They dragged Paul out of the Temple and tried to kill him. Trophimus later became ill at Miletus.

See the story of Trophimus in Acts 20:3-5; 21:27-29; and 2 Timothy 4:20.

Key event

Paul's third missionary journey; the early church

Tychicus (tik-i-kuhss)

Tychicus was a missionary who traveled with Paul. Paul called him a "much loved brother." Tychicus often carried letters and messages from Paul to the churches. Paul sent Tychicus to encourage them and let them

know how Paul was doing. Tychicus was a reliable helper whom
Paul could depend on to do the work he asked him to do.
**See Paul's words about Tychicus in Colossians 4:7-9;
Ephesians 6:21; 2 Timothy 4:12; and Titus 3:12.**

Key event
Paul's third missionary journey; the early church

Uriah (yur-**eye**-uh)

Uriah the Hittite was one of King David's faithful mighty men called the Thirty. Uriah was a selfless man and a skilled warrior. In fact, he fought bravely for David during a war against the Ammonites. His death is one of the Bible's saddest stories. Uriah was Bathsheba's husband. But David wanted Bathsheba for himself. Sadly, David took her from Uriah while Uriah was out fighting. He then sent a letter to his army commander telling him to put Uriah in the front line of fighting so that he would be killed in battle. David's awful plan worked. But the prophet Nathan exposed David's sin, and David and Bathsheba's first child died. **See Uriah's sad story in 2 Samuel 11:1-25 and 23:39.**

Key event
Reign of David

Uzzah (uz-uh)

Uzzah was a man killed for touching the Ark of God. The Ark had been kept in Abinadab's house for 20 years. Abinadab was Uzzah's father. King David wanted to take the Ark back to Jerusalem. He and the people were celebrating as they went. But David did not follow God's instructions on how to move the Ark. He put it on an oxcart instead of carrying it with poles. When the ox stumbled on a rough spot, Uzzah reached out his hand to steady it. Uzzah was trying to help, but he was not sup-posed to touch the Ark under any circumstances. God struck him dead right there beside the Ark.

See Uzzah's story in 2 Samuel 6:1-7; 1 Chronicles 13:7-14.

Key event
Reign of David

Uzziah (uh-zye-uh)

Uzziah, or Azariah, was a mighty king of Judah who became proud and tried to offer incense on the Lord's altar. He became king when he was 16 years old and reigned for 52 years. Uzziah had a strong army and brought power and prosperity to Judah. At first he obeyed God and asked for God's help. God gave him success. But then Uzziah became proud and was unfaithful to the Lord. He went into the Temple to burn incense on the altar. The priests told him he was doing wrong and must leave. But Uzziah would not obey. As he stood there, the Lord afflicted him with leprosy on his forehead.

See Uzziah's story in 2 Chronicles 26:1-23.

Key event

Reign of Uzziah

Vashti (vash-tee)

Vashti was the wife of King Ahasuerus, also known as Xerxes I, and queen of Persia who was deposed when the king had a banquet for all his nobles and officials. The men were drinking a lot of wine. Queen Vashti held a separate banquet for the women. After seven days the king commanded Queen Vashti to go to his banquet and show off her beauty and crown. The queen refused. King Xerxes was furious and asked his advisors what he should do. They feared all wives would disrespect their husbands. So they told the king he should get rid of Queen Vashti and get another queen. That's what he did! He chose the Jewish woman, Esther.

See Vashti's story in Esther 1:1–2:4.

Key event
The Exile

Witch of Endor (wich uhv en-dor)

The witch of Endor was a woman who practiced the black arts of sorcery and divination. She did not trust God for her knowledge. King Saul had banished witchcraft from his kingdom. But this woman still secretly practiced witchcraft. King Saul was worried about the Philistine army that was preparing to fight him. He disguised himself and went to the woman's house. Saul asked the witch to contact the prophet Samuel who had died. This was against God's law. Usually the woman tricked people; she did not really expect to see Samuel appear. But this time Samuel did appear, because God intervened. The witch was very scared.

See this story in 1 Samuel 28:1-19.

Key event
Reign of Saul

Zacchaeus (zuh-**kee**-uhss)

Zacchaeus was a chief tax collector for the Romans who became a follower of Jesus. He was a Jew and very rich. Among the Jews, tax collectors were seen as traitors because they worked for the Roman government. Not only did they take money for taxes, but they took extra for themselves. Jesus went to Jericho where Zacchaeus lived. Zacchaeus was a short man so he climbed up a sycamore tree to see Jesus as he passed by. Jesus went home with Zacchaeus. Jesus' love for Zacchaeus turned

Zacchaeus' heart to God. Zacchaeus gave half of his riches to the poor. He also paid back four times the amount he had cheated out of others.

See the story of Zacchaeus in Luke 19:1-10.

Key event
Jesus' ministry

Zechariah (zek-uh-**rye**-uh) (the prophet)

Zechariah was a prophet to the people in Jerusalem after they returned from exile. The people had been in Babylonia. They returned and were supposed to be rebuilding the Temple. But the people were not working on this important job. They also were failing to worship God. They were being mocked by their neighbors. But Zechariah encouraged the Israelites to do the work of rebuilding the Temple and return to God. Zechariah had visions of the first and second coming of the Messiah. Zechariah and Haggai were prophets at the same time.

See Zechariah's story in Ezra 5–6 and in the book of Zechariah.

Key event
The Exile; rebuilding of the Temple

Zechariah (zek-uh-**rye**-uh) (John the Baptist's father)

Zechariah was a Jewish priest who became the father of John the Baptist. Zechariah and Elizabeth, his wife, were old and had no children. Zechariah was serving in the Temple. Then the angel Gabriel appeared and told him that he and Elizabeth would have a son. They were to name him John. He would help turn people to God and make plain

189

the way for the Messiah. Zechariah had trouble believing this. So Gabriel said that Zechariah would not be able to speak until the baby was born. When the baby was born, friends thought he should be named Zechariah. Speechless Zechariah wrote, "His name is John" on a tablet. Then he was able to talk again, and he praised God with a song predicting the coming of the Savior. **See Zechariah's story in Luke 1:5-80.**

Key event
Birth of Jesus; birth of John the Baptist

Zephaniah (zef-uh-nye-uh)

Zephaniah was a prophet during the reign of King Josiah of Judah. Zephaniah was a prophet for 19 years. Some of that time, Jeremiah ministered also. The prophecies of Zephaniah were for Judah and all the nations. Zephaniah spoke of God's judgment and mercy. The message of judgment was not meant to say that God is always angry. It was meant to show people how important it is not to sin and to start doing what is right and good. The message of mercy promises that God will be kind to those who turn from their wrong and listen to God. Zephaniah wanted to give God's people a message of hope found in God. **See Zephaniah's message in the book of Zephaniah. Details of King Josiah's reformation are in 2 Kings 22:1–23:30.**

Key event
Reign of Josiah

Zerubbabel (zuh-**ruh**-buh-buhl)

Zerubbabel was the governor of the people returning to Jerusalem from exile in Babylonia. He led about 42,000 Jews back from Babylonia. They had been in exile for 70 years. Zerubbabel was a good leader. He emphasized the importance of worshiping God first. Then Zerubbabel and the people started rebuilding the Temple. But they were discouraged by those who wanted them to fail. The prophets Haggai and Zechariah encouraged the people to continue. Then Zerubbabel and the people completed the task. Zeubbabel was the son of Shealtiel and a relative of King David. He was also an ancestor of Jesus.

See Zerubbabel's story in Ezra 1–6. He's mentioned in Matthew 1:12-13.

Key event

The Exile; return from captivity

Ziba (zye-buh)

Ziba was King Saul's servant. After Saul died, King David appointed Ziba to care for Jonathan's son, Mephibosheth who was crippled. David had promised Jonathan he would treat Jonathan's descendants kindly. David told Ziba to farm the land and bring in the crops on the property that had been Saul's. It was all Mephibosheth's now. Ziba deceived David and said Mephibosheth was not loyal to him. So David gave everything of Mephibosheth's to Ziba. Later Mephibosheth told David that Ziba had lied. To settle the matter, David divided the property between Ziba and Mephibosheth.

See Ziba's story in 2 Samuel 9:1-13; 16:1-4; and 19:24-30.

Key event
Reigns of Saul and David

Zipporah (zip-or-uh)

Zipporah was Moses' first wife and the mother of their sons Gershom and Eliezer. She had six sisters and her father was Reuel, also called Jethro. Zipporah and her family were Midianites. Moses met them when he fled Egypt. God told Moses to return to Egypt to talk to Pharaoh. Zipporah and their sons went with Moses. On the way, Moses became very ill. He had not circumcised his son. Perhaps Zipporah did not want to do it because she was not Jewish. But circumcision was an important sign of God's covenant with his people. Moses had to follow God's laws if he was going to lead God's people. So Zipporah quickly circumcised her son and Moses got well.

See Zipporah's story in Exodus 2:15-22; 4:19-26.

Key event
Moses in Midian